King of the Mountain

Caitlin Press Inc.
8100 Alderwood Road,
Halfmoon Bay, BC V0N 1Y1
www.caitlin-press.com

Cover design by Vici Johnstone.
All photographs courtesy of Jack Boudreau unless otherwise stated.
Cover image of Grizzly Bear, (ursus arctos horribilus) female shaking, Great
Bear Rainforst, British Columbia, Canada, ©Stephen Harrington/All Canada
Photos image acp65092.

Printed in Canada

Caitlin Press Inc. acknowledges financial support from the Government of
Canada through the Canada Book Fund and the Canada Council for the Arts,
and from the Province of British Columbia through the British Columbia Arts
Council and the Book Publisher's Tax Credit.

 Canada Council for the Arts **Conseil des Arts du Canada**  BRITISH COLUMBIA ARTS COUNCIL

Library and Archives Canada Cataloguing in Publication

Boudreau, Jack, 1933-, author
    King of the mountain : more stories and memories from
BC's backcountry / Jack Boudreau.

ISBN 978-1-927575-42-0 (pbk.)

    1. British Columbia, Northern--Biography. 2. Human-animal
relationships—British Columbia, Northern. 3. Outdoor life—British
Columbia, Northern. 4. Frontier and pioneer life—British Columbia,
Northern. I. Title.

FC3845.N67B68 2014   971.1'8   C2014-900487-7

KING OF THE MOUNTAIN

MORE STORIES AND MEMORIES FROM BC'S BACKCOUNTRY

JACK BOUDREAU

CAITLIN PRESS

Contents

INTRODUCTION

I ask the reader to come with me on a journey to British Columbia's wilderness. Dare to let yourself face some of the truths about what is happening with the predator/prey balance, and how people with little or no bush knowledge are in control. Visit with an outfitter who has spent 26 years in the northern mountains. If Dave's story does not confirm a life of constant adventure for you, I suggest you check your pulse, because it must have stopped. Hear my own personal experiences as well as exciting, harrowing and hilarious stories from the ones who know it best: the guides, pilots, prospectors and old-timers from the wilds of BC.

A black bear feasting on cocoons. Photo Steve Schwartz.

PART ONE

PREDATOR VS. PREY

The extinction debate

After spending a good portion of my life living and working in the mountains of British Columbia, I feel the need to share some of my views on the balance between predator and prey. I challenge the opinions of some environmental groups and the harm they are causing the ungulate (hoofed mammal) populations. They often appear to side with the predators, and seem oblivious to the suffering of the victims, despite the proof of the slaughtering that goes on in the woods by wolves and grizzlies.

No doubt it is time to have a serious, sensible dialogue about wildlife, but in order to do that we have to have some facts. Some people believe our forests were teeming with large animals when the caucasians arrived on this continent. But the truth is, aside from bison that covered the plains by the millions, many areas were almost devoid of big game.

When the Overlanders came down the Fraser River in 1862, they found nothing along this pristine river in the line of big game. They were forced to eat whatever they found: chipmunks, birds, porcupines and even skunks. They were at the edge of starvation when they hit civilization at Fort George and Quesnel. Unknown to them, there were caribou higher up in the mountains, but the travellers were so weakened by their trying journey they didn't have the strength to climb up there even if they had known.

One of the problems was that there was virtually no feed for big game in the solid stands of forest I grew up in, aside from lichen that the caribou fed on. In some areas there was only devil's club on the forest floor, which is rather hard on the digestive tract. The ungulates were concentrated along old burns, the lakes, streams or alpine during the summer months. For many years hides were shipped from Saskatchewan to New Caledonia headquarters in Fort St. James because of the shortage of big game in central British Columbia.

So what changed that brought animals into the area in droves?

Throughout the years I have noticed naturalists puzzling over what caused the massive influx of moose into the interior of British Columbia shortly after 1900. In my view it was a direct result of the countless number of fires that burned the old forest and allowed new growth. Many of these fires were deliberately set by homesteaders, hunters and railway personnel in their attempts to clear the millions of trees that confronted their every move, along the endless miles of the right-of-way. As well, prospectors and miners burnt off huge areas so they could access the ground more easily, the Dog Creek area south of Fort St. James being a classic example of this. They were also assisted by the First Nations people who learned the hard way that without fires, starvation was their lot.

This new growth resulted in a massive influx of moose. With the moose came their deadly nemesis—the wolf packs. Soon the wolves discovered a new prey source and attacked the caribou herds with such abandon that caribou were pushed to the edge of extinction in many areas. Wolf packs of up to 40 in number were reported to the wildlife branch, with the average pack size being about 15 to 20.

During the 1950s, the Game Branch conducted a huge poisoning program that drastically reduced the wolves' numbers. Now the packs have rebuilt and it will be interesting to see how the wildlife managers deal with this problem in the future.

And what about grizzly bears? Some people say there were far more grizzlies before guns appeared on the scene. This may be true of the plains grizzlies, but many other areas had few. As an example, my dad trapped, worked in the woods and packed supplies up to Grizzly Bear Mountain for guide Ben Sykes back in the 1920s. During his 30-plus years in the woods he saw a grand total of one grizzly bear.

Since that time, his sons have seen up to 20 grizzlies in one day around the same area. There is no question about it, there are far, far more bears now.

Several times I heard the old-timers tell about hearing thumping sounds in the woods, and when they investigated they found bears tearing old rotten trees apart searching for ants. It was tough pickings for many forest creatures back then.

We have serious problems out in the wilds, and it's partly because of the efforts of some environmental groups to hide the truth about wolves slaughtering the ungulates. Likewise, they continually play down the huge number of grizzlies and black bears that prevail at present. Therefore I must offer an alternative point of view.

Up until now, these groups have been stuck in first gear. Why? I believe there is something in humans that makes us side with the winners. If in doubt, take note of the attempts to destroy property and hurt others when our teams lose a lousy hockey or baseball game. The predators are the decided winners in the game of predator/prey balance.

Down throughout history there are endless stories that support the idea that the balance of nature does not work. Instead, the predators drive their prey to the point of extinction and then starve until their prey rebounds.

Anything we can do to assist the ungulates will benefit all of us in the long run. When we consider the wide range of enemies they have, it is a miracle any of them survive: wolf packs, grizzlies, black bears, cougars, trains, vehicles and even ticks that drive them crazy. And fair enough, the hunters too, but that is the only part of the equation that is controlled.

If we really care about the mountain goats, sheep, elk, moose and deer, then let's allow them to deliver their young in peace, and let the wildlife people and outfitters deal with the predators as needed.

Wolf control: A necessary evil?

Despite some popular opinion, an article in the *Vancouver Sun* dated November 16, 2012, states that BC's grey wolf population is on the rise and is currently sitting at approximately 8,500 wolves. Wolves are a formidable predator. The slaughter of ungulates by wolf packs has caused serious damage and has been proven over and over again.

Here are some facts:

In 2008 the Alaska Board of Game authorized their staff to shoot wolves from helicopters along the southern Alaska Peninsula, because caribou herds had dropped from 10,000 in 1983 to 600 animals by 2008. Almost no calves survived during the two years prior to the culling despite a pregnancy rate of 70 percent.

Studies done in the former Soviet Union showed that a single wolf can kill up to 50 domestic or wild caribou annually; a pack of two to five wolves can kill two caribou every three days. A continuation of this slaughter is being conducted at present in the Siberian Republic of Yakutia where over 16,000 domestic reindeer were destroyed last year. This was an unacceptable loss to the nomads caring for and dependent upon these animals for their survival.

Other studies in the Soviet Union showed that wolves bypassed the sick and injured in favour of well-fed ones, often focusing on the pregnant females. I know this to be true from personal experience.

During a three-week period in 1978 wolves attacked a seal population on the Caspian Sea. An estimated 17–40 percent of the seals were killed and left untouched.

The fight to control the wolf packs is a never-ending battle with tremendous expenses. To make matters worse, wildlife personnel and outfitters come under incredible pressure when they try to balance the prey-predator relationship as it pertains to wolves.

Some groups have concocted numerous myths to deceive the public, such as the nonsense that wolves increase wildlife numbers by taking out the sick and the weak. This idea may have originated in Africa by people watching lions in action, as lions are not able to catch much of their healthy prey because the prey are too fleet of foot. However, wolves are not like lions. They are able to catch most of the available prey, winter or summer, under any circumstances. They are persistent and keep after them. At times they will harass and injure their prey and then leave them for a while. When their prey stiffens up they return and pursue them to an obvious conclusion. So ask yourself if they take the sickly; then ask yourself if you would take a scrawny, sickly chicken home for dinner, or the choicest pick of the lot?

This has been proven a lie countless times. And let's remember that delivering mothers and their young are among the weak and are most often the victims.

The killing sprees wolves go on are not addressed by the wolf-lovers. In my first book, *Crazy Man's Creek*, I interviewed many of the pioneer trappers and woodsmen concerning this subject. They spent their lives in the woods and were totally honest.

Pioneer horseman Skook Davidson raised horses in the Kechika Valley from 1939 into the 1980s. He lost many head to wolves the first few years until he had to bring the populations down with strychnine, an unfortunate solution to a serious problem. Strychnine remains toxic in the body of the dead animal, so when other animals eat it, they too become poisoned.

Dave Wiens is a retired outfitter who owned the guiding area east of Skook's ranch at Terminus Mountain. His staging area was Toad River on the Alaska Highway, which is just south of the Yukon Boundary. Dave retired from the outfitting business and therefore has no axe to grind. I had a conversation with him about wolves, because I recalled the problems he had with them in prior years.

"That was our worst problem," he said. "We spent all winter trapping, snaring and shooting them. The Game Department seemed to turn a blind eye to it at the start, but it must have been obvious that if we didn't deal with the wolves, there would be nothing."

I asked if he was involved when they hunted wolves from the air, because I remembered the go-round in the media when that took place.

"Yes, I was involved in that, along with Fish and Wildlife. We bought a trapline and leased other traplines so we could get in there and deal with the wolves. That was 1983 or '84 when the moose calf crop survival rate dropped to 5 percent. This forced us to take action. It was ridiculous. Everywhere we went we found dead cows and dead calves. Finally our biologist, John Elliott, helped us get things going. I have to give him a lot of credit because he sure took flak over it all.

"We got a program going and raised a couple hundred thousand dollars in the States through the Sheep Foundation and the Safari Club. Several outfitters donated their planes, so we went in with three planes with pilots, spotters and skinners, while Fish and Game came in with the helicopter.

"The planes would locate the wolf packs and call in the helicopter to take them out. Sometimes we cleaned out an entire pack. We took out 500 wolves the first winter and the moose calf survival rate jumped to 35 percent. We took out another 500 the second winter and the rate jumped to 70 percent. That was in addition to the wolves we trapped, snared and shot. The game populations just exploded and for several years you could not find a wolf track in some of our areas.

"We did a good job for a while but we began to notice the wolves were adapting and changing their breeding patterns. When we first started hunting wolves there would be hardly any pups. For instance, there would be six adults and two pups. A year later it would be two adults and six or eight pups. A year or two after that it would be three adults and 10 or 12 pups; both bitches had pups at the same time, so they were just multiplying like rabbits. But we had to do it; we poured thousands of dollars into it. There was no alternative—it was deal with them or go out of business.

"The largest pack was one we ran into along the Muskwa River in 1982 or '83; it was a pack of 32 wolves. We saw lots of packs of 10 or 12.

"But they have advanced since that time in that the guides have really learned how to use snares. They gather up road-killed moose and drop them into areas where creeks meet and the wolves travel. They put them into willow thickets and then snare up the whole area. You put 30 to 50 snares in there and then come back later and pick up the wolves. That system has become quite efficient and it manages to keep more of a balance between predator and prey."

I couldn't resist asking if they ever caught any other creatures in their snares.

"Once in awhile we caught an elk or moose in one, but not very often. I remember catching an eagle in a snare. It was just sitting there like this, staring at us and it was a big bald eagle. We threw a coat over it, took the snare off and carried it to an opening where we let it go. It walked along the trail for a ways and then flew away; it wasn't even hurt. Another time we got a cow moose; it was just caught by its nose. It was walking along with its head too low and got caught. Every time we tried to get close to her she would rear up and strike, so Barry Clark—the fellow working for me—kept trying to get the snare off with a long stick. The moose finally got used to him and settled down so he managed to get it off. The odd time we did find one dead, but then we had another carcass to work with. It didn't hurt the ungulate populations any, but it sure helped to control the wolves.

"One thing for certain, every day was an adventure out there. It was always one thing or another."

Suddenly a memory came alive so I asked if he was up there when the Greenpeace guy, Paul Watson, was trying to stop the wolf hunts.

"Yes, one at Gary Vince's and another at our place. Whenever they would try to interfere at one place, we would move the operation overnight 150 miles to the other. They were always two steps behind us, and they had no way of finding us. So we would work that area for awhile and then move back again. We would get together with the helicopter pilots and a couple guys from the Game Branch. We were doing wildlife management. That's exactly what we were doing.

Two wolves on patrol. Photo Steve Schwartz.

"We spent six to eight weeks every winter doing that, so you can imagine how expensive it was. Just the cost of fuel was tough to eat. As well, we flew in terrible weather conditions, with winds that were hard to work in.

"Paul Watson's group was just up there that one year. He couldn't take it; he almost froze on that one trip. The people up north, especially Fort Nelson, wouldn't give him any sympathy so he had to leave. He had to accept the fact that he was in an enemy camp there, so that didn't last too long"

I interjected that I couldn't help feeling sorry for Paul Watson because of that debacle. I believe he meant well but had been terribly misinformed.

"The predators are the problem and it is tough to deal with the problem and stay within existing laws. Once we killed a pack of 32. Another time we killed 18 wolves in one fork of a creek, and the next day we went back and got another 12. And you know that malarkey about wolves having their own territory? That is not true because their territories often overlap. I can tell you that they will never get rid of the wolves, because that country is just too tough. The wolves are too smart and they travel a lot further than people may think.

"For instance, we tracked a collared lone wolf and it travelled 50 miles in one day, so that gives you an idea of their durability. We tracked one right into the head of the Racing River in the middle of nowhere, yet the next day it was back on the highway 50 miles distant and had just made a kill. There wasn't that much game up there so he came back to the highway where the game was.

"Toward the end it got better because we tried a new idea. We collared two wolves in each pack and tried to make sure we never shot them. The next year we went back in and quickly found them with the transmitters. But get this: by then they had new members with them. Four newcomers had joined up, so we had to take them out. This was really expensive, and it presented new problems."

I wondered aloud why people always seem to side with the predators. I asked Dave if he had any idea.

"I don't know. Perhaps it is because we are predators as well. We have our eyes in front of our heads just as all the other predators, but that's just a thought. In general, the public is unaware of the suffering the wolves inflict. When they are training their pups it is just a free-for-all; animals are torn apart and left crippled. It's a sickening thing to witness, but the public will not see it because the media will not show it. Not only is that their responsibility to make the public aware, but they could assist game management enormously by giving them the truth. They don't seem to have a problem watching African predators taking down a critter, so why not depict the true nature of wolves or grizzlies?

"The worst part of it all was dealing with the wolves. There were several traplines in our guiding area, and we ended up with trapping permission on a number of them. We bought the most significant one where most of the game spent the winters. One of my guides owned another line in our area so we could go there as well. We ended up with most of the lines in the guiding area. The purpose of the traplines, besides fun, was to control wolves and keep them in balance. It was a tremendous expense and we didn't break even, but what we did was set up a deal with our clients that if they sent us $500 for our wildlife management, we would send them a pelt. These pelts would be ready for taxidermy and would be either a wolf, lynx or wolverine. We ended up with numerous people supporting out management plan. Many of these were repeat clients who knew we were actively managing things and it was a place they and their children could come and find an abundance of wildlife.

"We had enormous expenses, such as the airplane, which cost between $125 and $150 an hour, so their help was sure appreciated. It was fun to go out there and find where the game was and how the animals were doing in the wintertime. That was where we really learned the endless struggle wildlife faces with wolves. Sometimes we would find a place where there would be kill, kill, kill, and then cow, calf, cow. It was ridiculous, so we tried to thin the wolves out. If we hadn't, they would have cleaned the place out."

Wolf trouble in Russia

Any person who loves an abundance of wolves should have been in the small town of Verkhoyansk, Russia, during 2011, when a huge pack of 400 wolves killed 30 horses in a period of four days. But that was just the opening salvo.

During January 2013, news was hitting the world concerning wolves slaughtering reindeer in Northern Russia. President Yegor Borisov of the Sakha Republic had just declared a state of emergency: "Reindeer herders are facing an onslaught of wolves from the forested areas. A suspected shortage of hares has created a nightmare for the herders. Squads of hunters will descend on the area on January 15, with the promise of six-figure salaries for the most successful hunters."

A sum of $1 million US had been approved toward the hunt, and they hoped to bring the wolf population down to 500 from the estimated 3,500 animals. During 2012 wolves savaged 16,111 reindeer, representing a loss of $5 million to the herders. As well, 314 domesticated horses were taken down. Figures showed that 730 wolves were killed during 2012.

The *Moscow Times* dated April 23, 2013, stated that the 620 hunters had killed 583 wolves since January. During that same period of time the wolves had taken down 2,600 reindeer and 167 horses. The hunters got 20,000 rubles per pelt out of the total 32 million rubles allotted for the 2013 season.

The elusiveness of the wolf packs was starting to hit home with a bang now. As many wolf hunters learned during the 1930s and '40s, hunting wolves for a living was often a one-way ticket to starvation. Now these Russian hunters are learning this same lesson, so they are talking about the use of helicopters, but once those are involved, the 32 million rubles ($1 million) will evaporate in a hurry.

Vladimir Kreve, head of the Biodiversity Program at the World Wildlife Fund stated, "The idea of killing 3,000 wolves is not feasible… even if they did, populations would recover quickly."

I believe he got it right, so the predator-lovers will be pleased to know that the wolves are winning hands-down in the battle to save the domesticated reindeer. Perhaps that news will deter the groups now organizing in England from trying to stop the wolf hunts in Russia.

The L19 lifting off Sheep Creek. Photo Dave Wiens.

It's a shame there are no groups organizing to protect the reindeer.

Several of the old-time trappers I interviewed told of the terrible slaughter of ungulates when the wolves were at their numerical peak in the 1940s and '50s. An example was told by Oliver Prather, who trapped the Slim Lake country for over 50 years. I quote:

"I was walking along Boulder Creek just east of Longworth, when I came upon some deer that had just been killed by wolves. The sign in the snow was fresh and easy to read. I searched around and in just a small area I found 15 dead deer. They had all been killed in a short period of time, in one frenzied killing spree."

Oliver told me that almost nothing had been consumed from the carcasses.

In about 1958 I interviewed Jack Carnasky of Dome Creek, BC, for my book *Crazy Man's Creek*. He trapped and prospected along the Torpy-McGregor Mountains from 1915 to 1924. I asked, "Do you feel that the wolf poisoning program was justified?"

He responded with, "Well, they certainly killed a pile of game. In a trip along the Torpy Mountains one fall, Chris, Frank and I came upon the carcasses of 16 moose and one caribou that were killed by wolf packs. In every case only a small amount of flesh had been eaten, usually only the noses, and they could have been eaten by other animals." It is my belief that porcupines dined on the noses of those carcasses.

For many years I believed the decline in caribou populations throughout Interior BC was mainly due to forest fires and logging the old-growth forests. I now believe the wolf packs were the main culprits, with logging playing a much later, secondary role.

Ole Hansen trapped and guided the McGregor watershed for over 50 years. He described how he first started hearing the wolf packs in that area in the late 1920s. They were always up around timberline so it should be obvious they were after caribou.

Farley Mowat's dangerous misconceptions

I often wonder if Farley Mowat had any awareness of the harm he did to the ungulates with his book *Never Cry Wolf.* He states that two common misunderstandings are that wolves do not kill more than they can use, and that they do not kill for fun, the latter being one of the main differences that separates the wolf from the man.

Mowat destroyed his credibility with many of the woodsmen I queried by making those two statements. There is abundant evidence by scientists, as well as woodsmen in general, that wolves go on killing rampages. This is especially true while they are teaching their young how to hunt. I love Mowat's writing, but this book just didn't appear to make sense.

After *Never Cry Wolf* came out, Canadian Wildlife Federation official Frank Banfield compared it to *Little Red Riding Hood* stating, "…both stories have the same factual content."

A wolf expert named David Mech stated that in all his studies he had never encountered a wolf pack that primarily subsisted on small prey as shown in Mowat's book.

When I first read the book I thought it was a complete fabrication. It stands to reason that he had at least one camera with him on that expedition, yet there is not one wolf picture in his book. Could Mowat have destroyed them when someone pointed out that he had actually been studying coyotes? But that presents another problem—since there are no coyotes in the Barren Grounds, where did he study them?

I have never seen or heard of wolves catching mice in the manner he suggested. But coyotes do; in fact they catch mice exactly as Mowat described. They are perfectly designed to hunt mice, and can live on small creatures as his studies supposedly showed. One need only watch coyotes in fields during early morning or evening to realize they have raised the hunting of mice to an art form. Coyotes hunt mice with their front paws, while, to the best of my knowledge, wolves hunt with their teeth. I once watched a fox diving head-first into the snow to get mice; just like coyotes, they seem to pinpoint their presence with great accuracy.

I discussed this book with other woodsmen, and like them, I finally gave up trying to make sense of it.

I strongly feel that in the interest of public awareness the media should show the real picture of the slaughter out in the woods. It could change the public perception and allow the people involved to deal with the predators in a necessary and appropriate manner without constant interference.

A word from the experts

During November 1999 the University of Northern BC in Prince George sponsored a symposium by its Natural Resources Society. Among the speakers was Dale Seip, a habitat specialist with the Ministry of Forests. He discussed how the ministry had attached radio collars to moose, caribou and wolves to study their interactions in the Quesnel–Wells Gray Park area. "We have a large number of adult caribou being killed by wolves," he said. "During the late 1980s almost a third of the adult female caribou were being killed every summer." Seip also showed that the caribou calf population suffered heavily when wolves were in the area. In fact, less than 10 percent survive. He supplied statistics showing that the calf population went from 220 in 1986 to 90 in 1993. There are countless other studies showing similar results, but the message does not get through.

The proof is out there. In the United States, Congress has just passed a law allowing the hunting of wolves in Idaho and Montana, where the wolf packs are expanding and the elk herds are diminishing. Regrettably, the same battles have to be fought over and over again.

There does appear to be some light at the end of the tunnel in the never-ending battle with the wolves, as shown in the following study sent to me by biologist Mark Williams.

Wolf sterilization has been used in two previous caribou recovery programs. Up to 15 wolf pairs were treated on the summer range of the Fortymile caribou herd in Alaska, in conjunction with live translocation of subordinate wolves, and winter trapping. Herd size grew from about 22,000 to 45,000 caribou over eight years, the first increase in the Fortymile herd in decades. Up to six wolf pairs were sterilized in the Aishihik area during three to five years of intensive aerial control. Sterilization substantially reduced wolf rate of increase in later years, while caribou abundance continued to rapidly increase.

There are other similar wolf trials in operation, such as the sterilization program underway in the Quesnel Highlands where the mountain caribou have been declining for years. Just how effective this program will be should be known in two or three years, but so far it appears to offer some hope.

Growing numbers

Perhaps the reader was lucky enough to see the photograph taken by Travis Tzakis along the headwaters of Hawkins Creek east of Yahk, BC. This picture was on the internet for some time during early 2012 and was taken just north of the US border. It shows a pack of 25 wolves travelling in single file. It is certainly understandable that by alternating lead trailbreakers a large pack can travel long distances in a single day, even in deep snow conditions. This is the first time in the last 60 years that I have heard of a pack of wolves numbering more than 20. However, I have been in contact with David King, a naturalist/biologist in Prince George who states that a few packs southeast of the city have now reached this size.

Prince George Game Inspector Walter Gill told me that he had evidence of a large pack of wolves travelling about 70 miles in one day and night in midwinter. Just picture a poor moose having to face a pack such as this, especially if the moose was floundering in chest-deep snow with a crust that supported the wolves.

Travis stated, "You wonder why there are hardly any moose left and the deer and elk are in trouble. We transplant caribou for these guys to wipe out."

I think Travis got it right. The statement he made is echoed over and over by our wilderness guides. If they did not take matters into their own hands and deal with the wolves, there would be no point in continuing guiding because there would be little in the way of wildlife left for their hunters after the wolves.

While I am on the subject of wolves, I must relate a story told to me by my brother Clarence. After the wolf poisoning programs of the 1950s, the moose population increased. For example, on May 18, 1965, Clarence came by motorboat from the town of Sinclair Mills to Penny with Arnold Prather in his riverboat, a distance of 37 miles. Along the way they saw a total of 18 cow moose, some with calves that had just been born and others in the process of being born. These moose like to have their young near the water or on an island in the river so they can swim in the case of a predator attack, especially by bears.

Here is another fact for the predator-lovers to chew on. When wolves chase ungulates for any great distance in cold weather, they do not have to kill them outright. They just have to bide their time for a few days and return to the scene to find their prey down and helpless with pneumonia.

Perhaps the most surprising part of the wolf phenomenon is how they can be so intelligent on one hand and yet so short-sighted on the other. Time after time they slaughter their prey until they face starvation; then as a last resort, they have been known to eat their own young until game populations increase once again.

An example of this was supplied to me by John Patrick, a CNR section foreman stationed in Penny for many years. Take note that this was just a few years after the wolf packs had been decimated using poison.

It was the late 1950s, and he had just taken his motor car off the track to wait for a passing train. As he and his three crewmen waited in silence, their attention was drawn to some noise on the hillside above them. Four wolves were making their way down the slope through the deep, loose snow when the three largest wolves attacked the smallest one. The men shouted and banged things to such an extent that the wolves broke off their attack and made their way down across the railway track to the Fraser River. For several minutes the crippled wolf licked its wounds and then dragged itself along their trail down onto the ice of the frozen river. Although the men could not see what happened, the yelping started up again for a minute or so and they assumed it had been killed and devoured.

I recall driving the Yellowhead Highway in about 1970. When I got to a spot six miles east of Tabor Ski Hill, the wildlife officer I had been following pulled over and parked. I thought he wanted me to stop so I pulled over behind him. He was not interested in me, though. Rather, he had spotted a flock of ravens a short distance off the road and was instantly suspicious. I walked with him to what turned out to be a wolf-killed moose. It had obviously been killed that same day, because the tracks were fresh atop an overnight snow-fall. The pack had already fed, and perhaps they heard us coming on the crusted snow and left the area.

The officer bent over and retrieved a part of the moose that had not been eaten. It turned out to be the fetuses of two calves. The pack had taken down three moose rather than just one. The officer did not appear too pleased with the situation. It struck me that the laws of nature are not always pleasing to the human eye.

If, like me, people want to see our forests come alive with an abundance of ungulates and birdlife, then there must be continuous human intervention and predator control.

Human encounters with wolves: Too close for comfort?

Roy Sinclair spent most of his 75 years in the mountains logging and trucking and he worked a trapline in the Flathead country south of Fernie, BC. Here is one of his wolf stories.

"The logging had closed down for the Christmas holidays, so I had time to walk up the mountain behind home whenever I wanted, which was nearly every day. As there had been little snowfall that winter, I could cross the stream above our home on a little foot-bridge and climb to a logging road. This was a solid form of exercise which was intended to keep me in shape.

"One day I had climbed up and was walking along that road in six inches of old, lightly crusted snow with two inches of powder on top. My steps were going, *crunch, crunch.*

"It seemed loud to my hearing, but the powder may have muffled it somewhat. The wind was at my back and moving faster than I was, meaning any wild animal with half a nose should have known I was coming before I got there. As I walked around a bend, I came upon two silver-grey wolves lying on the edge of the road, basking in the sunshine. The closest wolf, about 80 feet from me, was licking and nipping at one of its paws, much as a puppy does. The other wolf, about 50 feet further, appeared to be half-asleep. I stopped in full view of them and just watched for perhaps five minutes and that is a long time. One of them arose and started looking nervous, so I said, 'What are you guys doing today?'

"I had their full and undivided attention for about 10 seconds and then they started making tracks, and quickly too. There seemed no explanation for my getting so close to them, except that they had scented me every day, and saw my tracks as well. I finished my walk and went home.

"The following three days it was the same thing—they followed my tracks around each time. One morning as I left the house, I found their tracks just beside Betty's greenhouse, so I followed them up the mountain. Then I missed two days and when I went back up again they were gone. So, do they have a massive sense of humour or are they into one-upmanship?"

Readers may remember Steve Schwartz, professional canoeist and naturalist, from my previous book. He paddled from Rocky Moun-

A necessary wolf kill. Photo Dave Wiens.

tain House, Alberta, to Montreal's Expo 67 in the 3,283-mile great canoe race. Also, he and a partner did the canoe trip around the Bowron Lakes' chain in 14 hours and 52 minutes. That was excellent time for the 72-mile distance with its portages.

Steve spends an enormous amount of time in the woods, and has a huge array of top-notch wildlife pictures to show for his efforts.

As Steve is a man of endless patience, he often manages to get beautiful close-up pictures of wolves. He has noticed that one day a pack of wolves will have seven animals and a few days later the same pack may have nine. It is my belief that the wolves often break up into pairs while they are out scouting for prey.

Or perhaps some of them take a few days off to go partying; I know I met quite a few wolves at parties during my time. Har! Har!

Many of Steve's wolf pictures appear to be taken along waterways. It is a fact that wolves do indeed like to follow creeks and rivers. It makes sense, because much of their prey does likewise.

Options for wolf control

As you can see, this is a tricky subject, and there are wildly different opinions on how to deal with wolves. In 2010, BC's mountain caribou science team recommended the immediate aerial removal of wolves that are seriously threatening the caribou populations, but were met with disapproval from the public. Their goal was to increase the caribou population, estimated at 1,800 to 1,900 animals, to the pre-1995 level of 2,500 animals within 20 years.

Robert Serrouya, a member of the team, told the *Vancouver Sun* that it's a tough situation, but something needs to be done: "It does sadden us that some wolves and cougars will have to be killed to save these endangered caribou. Aerial gunning is the most humane way of removing wolves, compared to all other alternatives, and it also allows people to selectively remove animals that pose the greatest risk."

I believe wolf control should be continuous to keep the pack numbers low, and this will always require constant monitoring of quota adjustments.

But until the two sides can see eye to eye and work out a solution based on the facts, the ungulate population will continue to suffer and decline. I hope that day comes before it's too late.

BEARS

Let's keep bears wild

As much as we may not want to hear it, there are getting to be far too many grizzlies in many areas of BC. It is now common for hunters to have to abandon game animals because grizzlies have arrived on the scene. This was almost unknown when I was a lad; in fact, I only heard of one case where that happened and that was to my brother Joe and a friend about 1945. In that case, the mother grizzly had two tiny cubs and yet she only weighed about 100 pounds. She was starving and had no choice but to try to drive my brother off the moose he had shot.

But now, because of their increased numbers, all that has changed. Some wilderness outfitters state that if they can't get their animals out of the woods the same day, the bears are on them when they return. In brushy areas with poor visibility they usually put flags on the carcasses and if they see the flags are down, they concede defeat and the bears win. After all, they do not want their guides or hunters mauled or killed.

It is a fact that in areas where the wolves are being controlled, grizzly bears are having larger families, and I believe this is also directly related to logging. I have heard several reports of mother grizzlies with four cubs, which was unheard of in the past—at least in the interviews I had with the old-time woodsmen. Several of them told me they seldom saw mothers with three cubs. That fits in well with my own experiences prior to the increase in grizzlies after the wolves were poisoned off in the 1950s. The first time I heard of a family of five grizzlies (four young) was about 1990, when there were many reports from people along the Babine River who had spotted them. In fact, the bears had chased some of these folks away from the stream where they were fishing. In 2012, wildlife photographer Leon Lorenz shot some HD footage of four two-year-old (third summer) grizzlies travelling together on the West Torpy River.

Between 1993 and 1998, Bill Benedict and I took videos of 17 grizzlies in a one-mile area at the 5,000-foot level, and had all of them in view at once. We also took video of 26 different grizzlies in the same area in just over a day. A film crew from the US spent two days in these mountains and filmed 22 grizzlies in two days.

In Yellowstone Park, the whitebark pine, one of the grizzly's food staples, is dying off in droves because of pine beetle and blister rust attacks. These trees produce an abundance of seeds that are stockpiled by squirrels. The bears regularly raid these piles, which are a rich source of protein. The cutthroat trout—another food source—are also dying off.

Grizzlies aren't doing too bad for a threatened species.

Tragedy at Yellowstone National Park

Opposing forces have always been at war where grizzlies are concerned, and Yellowstone Park is no exception. After 24 years without a human fatality, all hell has broken loose.

Recently, a rash of bear attacks has caused park officials to re-evaluate their bear policy. In a seesaw battle, the grizzly bears have moved off and on the endangered species list. But here are some facts:

In June 2010, a 70-year-old botanist was found dead in Yellowstone from a bite to the head. The bear was tracked and shot from a helicopter.

A month later in the same park, a young man was camping with his girlfriend in the Soda Butte area when a grizzly attacked them in their tent. The man was bitten in the calf area and the woman awoke to a bear chewing her arm. She screamed repeatedly and noticed that the bear bit harder each time. At that point she played dead and the bear released her. When officers arrived on the scene they found the body of another camper. He had been dragged a short distance, then killed and partly eaten. The next day the bear returned and was caught and euthanized and her three cubs were sent to a zoo. Tests indicated she had existed almost exclusively on a vegetarian diet. No one could explain her attack on human prey.

On July 5, 2011, two hikers decided to hike the Wapiti Lake Trail. Along the way, they passed a sign that warned of bear country. The sign explicitly warned hikers not to run when confronted by bears. A mile into their hike, they met a grizzly with two cubs. When the sow spotted them, she attacked, and the couple made a terrible mistake by trying to run away. The bears quickly caught them and the sow laid the man low with a wicked swat to the head. She chewed him up a bit and then attacked the woman. Luckily, the bear bit her backpack and then ran off to her cubs. The man was dead on the spot. The official decision was that the sow had acted defensively, so no action was taken against her.

The park wardens were at a loss to understand why people repeatedly ignored the basic instructions on how to deal with bear attacks. The clear directive had warned them not to run, and justifiably so, because when you run you become their prey. As well, the mandatory bear spray would have been useless to them if they ran.

In that instance, in my opinion, they should have taken off their jackets and held them as high and wide as possible. This confuses bears, especially if you appear much larger than them. At the very least, the bears should slow up in order to size up what they are attacking, and then the required bear spray can be used more effectively. Also, in the case of mothers and cubs, I try coughing at them, making the same sounds they make. The mother bear assumes it is a larger bear that may cripple or kill them.

A few weeks after the attack on the couple, in fact just eight miles from the previous attack, the body of a self-professed grizzly expert was found partly eaten. Hair and scat found nearby contained

Large black bear. Photo Steve Schwartz.

DNA profiles that matched the sow and one cub from the previous death. As per guidelines, the sow was found, euthanized, and her cubs sent to a zoo. A park official pointed out the importance of taking the cubs out of circulation, being that the mother has taught them to kill and eat humans.

Officials admitted the sudden spike in bear encounters puzzled them. One inescapable fact was that people were ignoring the basic rules: never hike alone, make lots of noise, and carry bear spray. None of the people attacked had the required bear spray.

But a greater concern to me is that humans seem to be losing their fear of bears. After years of working in the bush and interviewing guides and hunters, it really worries me when I hear and see people saying bears are not dangerous. Not only is this misleading, but it is foolish and dangerous to underestimate the nature of a bear.

Challenging Charlie Russell: The dangers of habituating bears

Although some people may want to live with grizzlies, and can do so by means of captivity and food dependency, it has been my experience that grizzlies do not want to live with people. Often back in the mountains they would get our scent and leave the area when we were about a mile distant from them.

It bothers me a great deal to see the false images often given to our young people by those who would have them believe that *wild* bears should be tamed and are not dangerous. So, in the interest of public safety, I must respond with the following points of view.

On March 9, 2003, I attended the Living with Bears slideshow and lecture by Charlie Russell at the University of Northern British Columbia in Prince George. The filming had been done in the Kamchatka Peninsula region of Russia, which has the highest number of brown bears in the world, estimated at up to 15,000. (New estimates place the number at up to 18,000.)

Russell took possession of several orphaned brown bear cubs and placed them behind an electric fence, to protect the cubs and themselves from the bears he states are not dangerous. This took place in a high-density brown bear area and, to me at least, resulted in the demeaning sight of *tame* bear cubs reduced to the level of domestic cattle. During the presentation Russell mentioned that he had trouble with the Russian authorities.

The trouble he alluded to was a Russian ranger named Vitaly Nicolayenko. Vitaly was called in to view Russell's operation, and from the outset he bitterly disagreed with Russell's method of handling bears, contending that, "…feeding half-grown bears made them eager for human handouts."

Was Vitaly competent to make that call? Let us look at his record.

Vitaly was a Russian ranger in charge of the Kronovotsky Wildlife Reserve, and he admitted the isolation was overwhelming. One of his rangers committed suicide, while several more became alcoholics.

Another Russian ranger named Dobrynya spent 25 years working with Nicolayenko and the bears. He summed up his feelings this way, "A bear thinks only of his own needs; he never thought about me. I thought about him; I think we've lost."

Vitaly spent a total of 33 years studying and following these *wild* Russian brown bears, logging just under an average of 625 miles a year on foot. He developed an uncanny ability to track these creatures during the summer months. In fact, much like a dog following a scent, the bears were unable to shake him off their trails. His accumulated information from all those years of study supposedly will fill at least one hundred journals.

So let's look at the finished product of both the Russell and Nicolayenko experiments.

The end result of the Russell experiment was that upon his return to Kamchatka, all his *tame* bears from the previous year were dead.

The old saying "A fed bear is a dead bear" always comes true unless they are being held in captivity; there may just be a time-lag between the two events.

We can well imagine these poachers and hunters having these tame bears come running at them; they would think they were attacking rather than begging for food. The fact that they were in a sanctuary holds little significance, as poachers are not restrained by sanctuaries. Also, some of these bears may have wandered outside of the protected area, or have been driven out by boar bears.

Now let us take a look at his critic, Nicolayenko, to see if he fared any better. His critics in turn accused him of following the bears too closely; in one instance he had pictures of himself lying close beside a large boar. His critics claimed this would cause the bears to lose their natural fear of man, and it turned out they were right. During 2003, 20 of the bears Vitaly followed and imposed himself upon were shot. In his own way, Vitaly made the exact same mistake as Charlie Russell. Although widely respected for their work with bears, the end result was that their bears lost their natural fear of man and became sitting ducks for the poachers and hunters.

As for Vitaly Nicolayenko, his world of bear knowledge did not protect him in the end. During late December 2003 he was attacked and killed by a mid-sized bear he was following. An empty pepper spray can was found by his side in what appeared to be a futile attempt to ward off the attack. His half-eaten body was found at the scene.

The foregoing is one of the biggest surprises I have experienced in all my years of studying bears. How could a man with Vitaly's experience around *wild* bears not wonder why this bear was still out of its den in the snow at the end of December? Was it not obvious that the bear was starving or suffering from some malady that would not allow it to sleep? His failure to recognize the danger cost him his life.

Speaking for myself, I spent 25 years hunting grizzlies and then spent the next 25-plus years studying them in their natural habitat in the mountains. I can state outright that I learned more about the bears in one year of studying them than in all the years I hunted them put together.

One memorable event took place when a kindly gentleman named Harold Olson was attacked and killed by a grizzly. He was cutting trail when he was attacked and was found the next day sitting against a tree. He had died attempting to hold his face back in place.

It appeared that during the attack Harold struck the bear a blow with his axe on the upper neck, as a cut was later found by a Prince George taxidermist. The next spring I guided a man named Gord Ross, who got the bear. It was taken only three miles from where Harold was killed.

With all this experience and input from other woodsmen, I feel competent to challenge some of the basic assumptions in the following article.

In the March 2012 edition of *Reader's Digest*, Charlie Russell described his experiences with [tame] brown bears in Russia. He also elaborated on his knowledge of grizzly bears. Russell stated that on a trip to Alaska, he wondered why the grizzlies "…behaved aggressively toward gun-toters, but left the filmmakers alone."

This grizzly killed Harold Olson in 1971. Gord Ross and I got it in 1972.

This is the equivalent of saying that hikers could avoid a grizzly bear attack by carrying imitation cameras around their necks. On the chance that he may be right, let's test this theory.

A man who supposedly wouldn't hurt a fly was a Japanese American photographer named Michio Hoshino. Yet he was dragged from his tent, killed and eaten by a brown bear in the same Kamchatka region of Russia where Russell raised his tame bears. People camped behind an electric fence nearby listened to his agonized screams but were unable to assist because firearms were not allowed in that protected area. The area warden stated that he tried to talk Michio into camping inside the electric fence, but he refused.

Photographers are not exempt from bear attacks.

Then there is the case of photographer Jim Cole. He was attacked twice by grizzlies in Yellowstone Park. The first attack took place in 1993, which he survived. In 2007 he was again attacked in the Hayden Valley area; that time he was critically injured.

He forced himself to walk the three miles to his vehicle holding part of his face on. He lost his left eye and received damage to his right eye.

And don't tell wildlife photographer Leon Lorenz of Dunster, BC, that grizzlies don't attack photographers. Two years ago he had a close call when a mother with a yearling charged him at point-blank range. This attack was captured on high definition video, and showed that only the deafening roar of his .44 magnum handgun stopped her. Both bears retreated unharmed, but I'll bet their hearing is still impaired.

Let's also take notice that hikers are frequently attacked by bears. Are we to believe they can avoid attacks if they hang cameras around their necks? This misinformation seriously detracts from the work done by sincere experts laying out safe guidelines for dealing with bears. As well, it can set up the inexperienced for a mauling or worse. When dealing with fatal grizzly attacks, take note that the list of human deaths is incomplete. For example, look up the year 1926 and you will not find the name of Tom Meaney there. He was killed by a huge grizzly bear in the Upper McGregor River area (Herrick Creek). The story was carried in the *Prince George Citizen* dated April 1, 1926, and in several succeeding issues.

Be that as it may, according to statistics between 1980 and 2010, 32 people were killed by grizzlies in Canada and the USA. Many more were severely mauled and died a year or two later, so their deaths were not attributed to bear attacks. During that same period of time 28 people were killed by black bears. This does not include the many people mauled, including children.

Charlie Russell further stated he believed he could prove that humans can live peacefully with bears by simply treating them kindly.

If we give that a try, why not treat cougars kindly and see how they get along with our pets?

But the truth of the matter can be easily resolved by asking the First Nations people of this country why their ancestors had such a deep fear of grizzly bears. I know from experience that some of them would move camp if they found signs of grizzlies around the area.

On January 30, 1920, the *Prince George Citizen* carried an interview with a man named Joe Merrienne aka Sousa Thapage, who had been a boatman and packer for the Hudson's Bay Company.

Joe recalled a memory from years gone by of what he described as a big Native man named Freddie Bascar. Freddie and his two brothers were walking through the woods when they were attacked by a grizzly bear. When the bear finally left, the two brothers were dead and Freddie was seriously injured, yet these men posed no threat to the bears.

Grizzly charging photographer Leon Lorenz. Photo Leon Lorenz.

But don't take my word for it, check the history books. They are replete with stories of First Nations people and others being attacked by grizzly bears when they posed no threat whatsoever.

Relocating bears

Charlie Russell also attacked wildlife personnel for their abuse of bears while removing them from urban areas. I know some of the people who do this and they are dedicated to their work. Every possible avenue has been explored concerning this problem and no solution has been found. Transplanting bears does not always work. Often they are attacked by resident bears in the areas they are moved to. Therefore it is imperative that they not be moved into high-density bear areas. I would also like to know how many bears die after being tranquilized. That being said, it is better to move problem bears to remote areas, regardless of the outcome, since we don't want to euthanize them.

Some studies have shown that they try to return to their former range time after time, each time after undergoing a severe weight loss. Many times they are in such a hurry to return to their own territory that they do not feed, therefore after being transplanted several times they can die of starvation. In the interim they can become extremely dangerous and aggressive.

Now let us look at the Kamchatka Peninsula where the Russell operation was located. It is well known that licensed guides take an abundance of trophies each spring from Kamchatka. For example, during 2007, hunters killed 300 bears and poachers were believed to have shot another 600. That represents 6 percent of the estimated total bears in that region. Obviously taking this number of bears is bound to leave some orphaned bear cubs.

Russell acknowledged that there is a lot of poaching going on in that area. If that is true, what is the sense of protecting those bears for a year or two and then sending them out on their own? What he called "reintroduced to the wild," I call abandoned to the wild. Since the mother grizzlies are shot for their furs or for trophies, it is obvious that this takes place in April or May, before the cubs are old enough to learn the ways of the wild. And let us be honest—a man cannot teach bears the ways of the wild; he can only teach them the ways of the tame.

Bears kept in captivity are not able to range up and down the mountains to take advantage of the changing food supply, so when they are released, or abandoned to the wild, they have no knowledge of how to survive on their own, and are sitting ducks for tragedy. Russell admitted that the *wild* boar grizzlies kill some of these *tame* bears. I certainly believe that, especially if they have the hated scent of humans all over them. So in a sense, it seems that the long-term result of these ventures is to supply the large boars, the hunters and the poachers who are after gall bladders, with domesticated bears.

An acquaintance of mine has spent his entire life working with wildlife. When questioned, he offered a simple test to determine whether bears are held in captivity for entertainment purposes or for their own survival. In 2003 he stated, "If bears were raised with their survival in mind, a hands-off approach would be used, preferably with little or no bear-human contact. If used for entertainment purposes the hands-on approach would be used in order to get the close-up pictures and human-bear interactions. To put it simply, they are reduced to the level of toys for human entertainment."

When I questioned this wildlife officer about the end results of feeding bears, he cited countless problems and tragedies that have resulted from these actions. The evidence is overwhelming and irrefutable—people who tame wildlife are doing these animals irreparable harm. For that reason the experiments that were carried on in Kamchatka are illegal in Canada and the US, and rightfully so.

The reader may ask if I have any proof to support my views concerning habituated bears. That is a fair question, and as an example one need only read *The Mackenzie Experience* by Andrew Mackay to learn what happens to habituated bears. This study was conducted over a three-year period at the Mackenzie Landfill Garbage Site from 1992–95. This supplied convincing proof that transplanting bears does not work. By the time the study ended 63 of the 67 grizzlies involved were reported dead.

As for Kamchatka, the area is besieged with bear problems. During 2008 two platinum mining camps, Khailino and Korf, were surrounded and held hostage by 30 large brown bears. The two guards were killed and according to some reports, partially eaten by the bears, and pleas for help were sent to the outside world. A speaker for the camps, Victor Leushkin, stated, "These creatures have to be destroyed; once they kill a human they will do it again and again."

Responding to the pleas, the government sent in snipers to deal with the bears. With so much pressure to reduce the number of bears in that region, is it not apparent that these so-called conservation projects are working at cross-purposes to the government? And who ever heard of brown bears (which are relatives of grizzlies) travelling in packs before this? Does this not prove that the bear populations have outgrown their food supply?

If an experiment such as Russell conducted is to have any chance of being successful, it should be done with no direct bear-human contact, and it should take place in a low-density brown bear area. In their attempts to survive, the young bears should not have to compete with adult bears for the available food supply, or be chased by a larger bear every time they turn around. Under the best of circumstances it is tough enough for a young bear to find a range of its own.

One thing is certain, once bears become habituated, problems result, and therefore any person who tames a bear for whatever reason is doing incredible harm.

People who feed us the line that humans and bears can live together in harmony ignore two centuries of evidence to the contrary. Carried to its conclusion, we would have tame bears in all our towns and cities looking for houses or vehicles to break into whenever they smelled food, and just picture the traffic problems. A short visit to Churchill, Manitoba, when the polar bears invade will prove we do not want their problems. Alternatively, a visit to Jasper, Alberta, when the elk take over the town and the golf course shows what happens when *wild* animals become *tame*.

The bottom line is that wild animals should be left wild; it works best that way for all concerned.

Whenever people are mauled or killed, excuses for the bear's bad behaviour abound. Such was the case when Timothy Treadwell and his girlfriend, Amie Huguenard, were killed and eaten by a boar grizzly on October 5, 2003, in Alaska.

In that case it was suggested that the boar was from out of the area and didn't recognize Timothy, who had frequented the area for years. Don't believe it. You can bet your boots this boar grizzly had travelled that area many times throughout the years. A boar grizzly is a creature of habit and will often follow the same trails throughout his home range for his entire lifetime unless driven away by development. Timothy had frequented the Katmai National Park area for

13 years, so we can rest assured that the boar had made his acquaintance on several occasions.

So what was the reason for these deaths? That bear was hungry and being that the salmon season was over, he was probably looking for some extra nourishment prior to going to his winter den site. Also, it seems obvious to me that Timothy had lost all respect for these beasts; how else can we accept the fact that he put his tent right on their game trail? I mean, you shouldn't try to force a large bear to walk around you. That is a no-brainer.

So in summary, what was the final message an inexperienced person can take from Russell's lecture and slideshow? It is okay to feed bears. It is okay to pet bear cubs, and in some cases mama bear will let you sit with her cubs while she goes for walks. It is even okay to take food away from a bear while it is feeding—an action guaranteed to produce fatalities.

Don't feed the bears!

The public is given a Disney-type view of bears that can and does end in trouble. An example of this is the people who illegally feed bears in national parks. I have it from a park attendant that at times the bears don't want the feeding to stop, and in a few cases they have climbed into vehicles and forced the occupants to flee for their lives. This attendant also believes it has been this feeding of bears that has attracted them to the roadways where they are all too often killed by vehicles.

I spent a few weeks in the Khutzeymateen Inlet north of Prince Rupert, BC, manning the ranger station for BC Parks. This estuary is a favourite feeding spot for grizzlies because of the abundance of sedge. The Khutz became a protected area because the grizzlies were sitting ducks for hunters arriving in boats. The hunters could drift in with the incoming tide and be right upon the bears without making a sound.

This area is famous for viewing bears because the bears only have two options—accept the intruders or stop eating and leave.

Since grizzlies are extremely hungry in late spring, they have to do the latter. I don't have a problem with viewing from boats, as long as the tourists do not try to approach the bears on land. I know of one bear expert that was kicked out of that area because he wouldn't stop mingling with the grizzlies. In my view BC Parks got it right when they banned humans from having contact with these bears. If the Parks people ever allow mingling with these bears, just imagine the litigation when someone is mauled or killed.

It is always the same story—people going to salmon spawning areas to watch the bears. The bears are desperate to get these fish just prior to den time so they must put up with the intruders. Surely we can all agree that this mingling causes these bears to lose their natural fear of humans. It should be a priority to stop this.

Besides, this does not prove that man and bears can live together. It does prove that the designation "bear expert" is often used as a licence to torment wildlife. Surely we have enough pictures of bears to go around, so why not back off to viewing areas, preferably elevated and sound proofed so the bears are unaware of human presence. Let's allow the bears to feed in peace.

As Grizzly Adams (1812–60) and others have shown throughout the years, it is easy to tame grizzly cubs, but the end result is always sorrow for the bears, one way or another. In every case I researched or can remember, where bear cubs were tamed, the end result was bad news for the bears. Usually the best they received was a trip to a zoo. Most had to be destroyed, and in two cases I recall, in Penny and Legrand, BC, they were destroyed after they mauled children.

I also strongly feel that a bear expert should not hold yearling grizzlies in captivity when it has been established that grizzly cubs have survived alone from the age of seven or eight months, and black bear cubs from the age of as little as six months. However, these bears were not dumped or abandoned into high-density bear areas. Also, it is critical that the cubs have the mother influence throughout at least part of the summer in order to learn the ways of the wild.

I recall in 1973 or '74 a hunter shot a mother black bear in error, saying he wasn't aware she had cubs. (This can happen because a mother black bear will often cross an opening to be sure it is safe before returning for her cub(s), which she has left in seclusion.) When these cubs refused to leave their dead mother's side during the following three days, we contacted Regional Wildlife Biologist Ken Sumanik in Prince George. Acting on his advice we live-trapped and transported the two cubs to Foreman Flats and turned them over to a Mrs. Sawitsky, who often cared for injured birds and animals. But she was not a bear expert, so she did an intelligent thing by not confining the seven-month-old cubs. Instead, she let them roam freely about their 150 acres of land so they wouldn't become habituated. When the first snowfall arrived about six weeks later, the cubs dug in under a cottonwood tree by the Fraser River. The following spring they emerged from the den, and after exploring the area for a few weeks, they returned to the wild.

During my 55 years around grizzly bears I have noticed that there is a quality about them that gives them the right to be king of the mountains. As a young man, I remember watching a grizzly tear a moose carcass to pieces. The bear was unaware of my presence and

A sow grizzly looking for salmon. Photo Lou Siguenza.

as I watched him I noticed the wild look in his eyes—a look that went right through me. There was also an aura of power and the vitality that comes from being wild. As he appeared to look right at me, I felt shivers run up and down my spine. To say I was just impressed is a gross understatement.

By comparison, I have watched grizzlies in captivity and they are not the same animal. The wild look, or spirit if you wish, is gone from their eyes. My observations have told me that captive bears are mere shadows of their kin in the wild and spend hours walking in circles or lying down with despair and boredom written all over them. Imprisonment of bears is just that; it is wrong no matter how it is done.

Worth viewing are old images that can be accessed online from Exploration Place in Prince George. Many show bears kept on chains attached to objects out in direct sunlight. We cannot imagine the agony these creatures went through being forced to stay in the direct sunlight of May before they shed their winter coats.

I suppose it is apparent that I have strong feelings regarding the taming of wild bears. These feelings come from the accumulation of a great many studies by others, as well as my years of personal experiences. I can't help but feel that all the work done in establishing safe guidelines for dealing with bears is flushed down the drain by the idea that bears are safe. And all this at a time when many young people, such as tree planters and forestry personnel, are working in the woods with the constant danger of wild bear encounters. Is it right to send young, inexperienced people into the wilderness armed with this ridiculous, one-sided view of tame bears? People must realize that the Russell bears were tame, and how many tame animals bite the hands that feed them?

People need to be prepared for the danger wild bears can present. I have been reading blogs and tweets that say things like: "...But Canadian Charlie Russell spent 10 years living with them [bears] in the Russian wilderness to prove that they aren't ferocious at all."

Where is the reality in all of this? What has working with tame bears got to do with the wild? And where are they going extinct?

We need to admit the truth that there are more grizzlies in many places than ever before in recorded history. The idea that the mountains are safe if you simply keep quiet and don't spread your scent is false information and is certain to cause injuries and death among the unsuspecting. I know I would not want it on my conscience.

Lately I have learned that there have been at least five more human deaths from bear attacks in Kamchatka. In one instance a woman was attacked and eaten right in an urban area.

As well, on August 14, 2011, a 19-year-old girl and her father were killed by a brown bear; so much for the harmless bears. That being said, it is generally accepted that these brown bears are not nearly as vicious as their North American cousins.

One of the latest attacks occurred at the Russian submarine base when two young bears killed a man fishing off the dock. Witnesses called police, who hunted the bears down along the streets of town. Police patrol the streets of this base every spring in an effort to protect the citizens from hungry, marauding bears. Perhaps it is true, as some sources state, that the bear populations in Kamchatka have outgrown their food supply.

Over and over I have noticed that people are being blamed for all the bear problems in Kamchatka. Perhaps we should accept the fact that nature is sometimes to blame. When heavy rains caused the streams to rise so that the bears had trouble catching salmon, the poachers were blamed for taking too many salmon. At the same time, Russian fisheries personnel were stating that because of global warming, the salmon were avoiding their rivers and going further north to spawn.

Some years much of the feed the bears depend on, such as berries, suffer crop failures. Couple that with a poor salmon run and it can spell disaster for an over-population of bears. If it is true that there are too many bears in Kamchatka, then perhaps there is no easy solution. The bears are faced with two choices: starve to death in a winter den, or worse yet, spend a month wandering aimlessly through the deepening winter snow searching for non-existent food until they perish. This is a scene that has been witnessed many times.

Contrary to what the dreamers may say, nature is not always kind.

Getting real: Bears in BC

Dave Wierns had this to say about the current grizzly population: "As soon as we took out so many wolves and the ungulates flourished, the grizzly bears started multiplying like crazy. Then the quotas started going down on grizzly bears when they should have been going up, and now there are grizzlies everywhere."

I explained that I couldn't possibly agree more because I had noticed the exact same thing in the Grizzly Bear Mountain area, where my book of the same name pointed out that after the wolf kills of the '50s, grizzly numbers skyrocketed. Whereas in the '40s on a trip through that area I was lucky to spot even one or a family of grizzlies, in the '90s I often spotted 15 to 20 grizzly bears. I had to mention that I believed their range burning had a profoundly beneficial effect on the bears.

"Actually, on all the wildlife," Dave said. "But now they have all these bears and they can be worse predators than wolves. They can be really nasty. I'm not sure how they are going to deal with this problem."

I offered that the answer was obvious—they should change the quotas to deal with the new reality because in many places grizzlies have completely lost their fear of man. Years ago I had no fear whatever when dressing out a moose, but those days are gone. Now if you cannot get your game out of the woods the same day, you had better be careful because odds are, there will be a bear on it the next day or possibly even the same day. The sound of gunfire is comparable to a dinner bell.

"I can give you another example, Jack," Dave said. "One of my guides had a hunter with him that got an elk late in the day. They field dressed it and then headed back for camp. They went just a short distance and ran into a grizzly on the trail. It had heard the gunfire and was coming to lunch. The bear would not get off the trail so they had to. The next morning they returned to the site and of course the bear had taken it over.

"But I feel that the biggest problem is that many people in the cities have no knowledge whatever about wildlife, and the politicians have to respond to their wishes. Therefore the Game Branch won't back you at all."

I agreed with Dave and then had a thought that perhaps the outfitters had to do a better job of informing the public that they husband the game populations and would quickly be driven out of business if they didn't.

I also pointed out that I hear people say that the regulations should be changed regarding moose because there are not enough bulls to service the cows. In reality I have never believed that was the problem; the predators have always been the problem.

I mentioned that many times when I was following the rivers I found black bears following moose with their newborn. In a few cases I deliberately interfered and drove them off.

Dave agreed. "We had one right on our ranch. An elk had just dropped its calf, and along came a black bear with its nose on the ground. I was out in the field fertilizing when I saw the cow running along the field and into the woods, so it appeared that she made it to safety. Then the bear came out and went right after her. In about ten minutes it got her calf. We shot a lot of bears right around our ranch, and only because we had to. That's why they have two calves. They often calf out at about 120 percent and maybe end up with a 20 or 30 percent survival rate. That is the predator kill rate in spades. When we took out all those wolves, everything came to life. Birds, and even the ptarmigan; there was game galore. There were little pockets of elk before, but after we hunted wolves in winter and burnt mountains in spring, the elk populations actually exploded. This shows that man has to interfere at times."

I agreed, and stated that one only needed to read the history of the north. Many of the woods wanderers told of how they walked 60 miles on snowshoes without finding a moose track. Yet they did find sign where the packs travelled in their relentless search for moose. Those people were not liars. They often faced starvation as the First Nations people did because they had no means to deal with the wolves.

"Sometimes the Forest Service was involved with the burns," Dave explained, "but other times folks just did what had to be done. The effect on the wildlife was almost unbelievable. Our hunters couldn't believe the amount of game in our area. They would often see 100 animals a day, and as many as 30 bull elk.

"I was just recalling an interesting experience I had with outfitter Stan Simpson in the Northwest Territories. We were going up the Keele River in his boat when we spotted a big bull caribou standing in the water. When we got closer, we saw a grizzly standing in the water about fifteen feet from the caribou. We drove up within a few feet of the bear before it took off. I guess it was waiting for the caribou to freeze up, and maybe that would have worked because he slowly walked out on the shore and just stood there. We walked up the mountain and kept looking back and he just stood there. When we came back down the mountain the caribou was finally gone, so we don't know if the bear got it or not."

Here's an article in the *Rossland Telegraph* by Andrew Bennett dated July 18, 2012:

> A cute cinnamon-coloured black bear had captured the hearts of many in Rossland, but was also causing more and more trouble. Two short months after the bear came to town, conservation officers (COs) were forced to put her down.
>
> "She showed up in town around mid-May," said Rossland Bear Aware coordinator Sharon Weider. "She was small, not much bigger than a dog, so people thought she was an orphaned cub."
>
> In fact, COs have recently confirmed that the bear was five

to ten years old and probably a runt; although she may have been in town in previous years, this was the first year she was noted as a problem.

"The bear was very comfortable in town… perhaps too comfortable," Weider said. "I got phone calls from people in different areas of town. The bear was out at all hours of the day and not paying any attention to people at all. This underscores the fact that the longer bears are tolerated, as they get older, they get bolder."

This bear caused continuous problems, including entering a home and cleaning out the fridge. After the bear was euthanized Weider made this statement: "When it reaches this point most hope is lost. Relocating the bears, even a great distance, rarely helps. There is little to no hope of changing the bear's habits to return to a wilderness diet."

This was a classic example of the destiny awaiting a habituated bear. Their ending is foretold with the beginning. As for it being a runt, the fact it was habituated may have meant it often went without adequate nutrition.

Since many people refuse to admit that sometimes there are far too many bears, especially black bears, countless problems ensue. Never do we hear any of these groups suggest the bears need to be thinned out, even when it is the only obvious solution.

Steven Herraro, of the University of Calgary, puts the black bear numbers at 900,000 in North America. Should we try for even more? It has reached the point where well-meaning groups such as Bear Aware are pushing people to refrain from letting their fruit trees ripen. "Get the fruit and berries off the trees as soon as possible" is their cry.

I suggest they watch migrating birds in both the fall and spring of the year. Their very existence depends on these berries that stand out so visibly after the leaves have fallen. Since humans have taken over so much of their wild lands, perhaps it is not asking too much that we leave a few berries for their meagre survival.

What comes next? Since grass is a favourite food of bears, will lawns be banned? Will farmers have to electrify their clover and oat fields? In fact, they would have to electrify their entire ranch to protect their stock. Experience has taught me that bears will always wander when their food supply runs low, especially in the fall of the year, and this includes into urban areas; nothing we do will prevent it, unless we all live inside electrified communes. This means that we either accept bears wandering around urban areas, with the nightmare world this will present, or deal with it.

So when some lady calls for help because a bear is in her kitchen (this has happened many times) or eating one of her pets, let's not get on the backs of wildlife personnel called to deal with these situations as necessity warrants.

Some thoughts on instinct

Let us take note of what Mark Twain put to paper regarding "instinct" in *What is Man*: "Now my idea of the meaningless term 'instinct' is that it is merely petrified thought, solidified and made inanimate by habit; thought which was once alive and awake but it became unconscious—walks in its sleep, so to speak."

For many years I have had to suffer the accepted doctrine that animals act or react out of instinct; my version is rather different. I believe that "instinct" is not an explanation. Rather, it is a cop-out. My dictionary defines instinct as, "...to act without conscious intention; innate impulsion; unconscious skill; intuition."

Perhaps the biggest surprise I experienced while studying wildlife occurred while studying grizzly bears. Throughout the years we often had grizzlies roar perhaps 10 or 12 times in the mountains. This always occurred around timberline, or in the subalpine. Never did I hear this roaring in the low country or along rivers unless the animals were wounded.

The first time I started getting suspicious was when a group of us were in the mountains and some grizzlies started roaring in the subalpine valley perhaps 400 yards below us. This took place after dark, and I noticed that a tremendous downdraft was taking our scent down to them. I also had pioneer woodsmen tell of similar experiences, but we all chalked it up to coincidence, or a fight between two bears. Prior to that event, I never even considered the possibility that these bears could be doing this on purpose.

Then, during September 1997, Bill Benedict and I were in the mountains watching grizzlies and we had to accept a truth. We had just got back to our cabin when we spotted a mother grizzly with two young climbing the ridge toward the place where we had just walked. When the bears hit our trail, the mother stood up and let out 12 long, loud roars and then they ran away from the area. That day we had seen about a dozen grizzlies, but the next day we glassed the entire area and the bears were all gone. Without a doubt, that mother had warned the other bears that hated humans were in their area. These bears have figured out just how vulnerable they are in the subalpine and have reasoned out a way to counteract it. Once I accepted this fact, I thought back to other times I had heard that amount of roaring in the mountains and it fit perfectly.

This, my friends, is far beyond instinct.

Something that has puzzled me for many years is how we would find an abundance of bears one year, and yet the next year there appeared to be only a few bears. That occurred a couple of times throughout the last 60 years. For many years I assumed they starved in their dens. These last years I have had lots of time to reminisce, so I want to offer another possible explanation.

In the late 1970s we had a silver thaw in the Penny area where I lived. It rained for a few days with the raindrops freezing on the trees and snow. The trees became so laden with ice that many poplars trees broke under the stress. At the same time there was a one-inch crust of ice atop the snow. If memory serves me, I believe this icy situation lasted for a considerable length of time.

My question is this—did the animals die in their dens for lack of oxygen? Was there enough ambient oxygen in the surrounding snow to

Cabin and horse corrals at one of Dave Wiens' guiding camps.

keep them alive? About that same time the marmots disappeared in the surrounding mountains. Where there had been colonies of them whistling at us, suddenly there was only silence. Is it possible that they were wiped out at that time? It may seem strange, but I thoroughly miss their presence. I used to love watching how they worked in unison with the Columbian ground squirrels to alert each other when danger threatened. When a coyote, eagle, bear, or wolverine happened along I could plainly hear their telephone system going to work.

Bear vs. Human: Attacks on the rise

Thank heavens there are still some people residing in the real world, because their observations and influence are desperately needed to counteract the misinformation so available today.

One such person is Steven Herrero. He stated that he has found that lethal black bear encounters are on the rise, and are more likely to occur in Canada and Alaska than in the lower 48 states. "Contrary to popular beliefs, the vast majority of black bear attacks don't involve the animals protecting their young. The black bear has evolved a dramatic repertoire of acts to protect their young, but they don't follow through. What surprised me was the disproportionate participation of males in the predatory side. Male bears, as opposed to females, have an instinctive need to be larger, and human beings look big and look like something good to eat."

Professor Herrero was quick to point out that, "Serious bear attacks remain rare and wilderness areas are relatively safe. But as humans have increasingly encroached on their habitat, the number of fatal attacks on humans by lone black bears has increased. In 110 years, 63 people were killed in 59 black bear attacks in the US and Canada, with 86 percent of those happening since 1960. Even though the lower 48 states are more heavily populated by humans, the most serious attacks are 3.5 times more common in Canada and Alaska. Some of the suspicions are that bears in the more northern environment are more food-stressed. Humans have not been a prey item over millennia, but now the bears are going to go for it. It is possible bears in northern regions are also less exposed to humans and the dangers they present."

Steven is considered an expert where bears are concerned, and it becomes instantly apparent that he has done an enormous amount of research. His book *Bear Attacks: Their Causes and Avoidance* is a must-read for wilderness types. His assertion that black bear mothers do not follow through on their attacks to protect their young is exactly what I learned many years ago. In my second book, *Grizzly Bear Mountain*, I described this exact thing. As foolish as it may seem, I used to deliberately get close to them just to see what the mothers would do. In some cases the mothers would huff, puff and fake charges, but always managed to keep brush or willows between us. In most cases they sent their cubs up trees and disappeared until I left the area.

And therein lies a major difference between blacks and grizzlies—where black bear mothers readily send their cubs up trees, as a rule, grizzlies do not. This is a tremendous pressure release and many attacks on humans would be avoided if only grizzlies would do the same thing. The only time I have ever heard of grizzlies doing this is when a guide who found grizzly cubs up in a tree saw a boar grizzly nearby. He felt that the mother sent them up to protect them from the boar. Another time was when a man was charged by a grizzly when he surprised her at close range. The mother was shot and the cubs climbed the tree of their own volition.

Jack hooking up a sling load. Photo Allan Spoklie.

But why should grizzlies have learned to send their cubs up trees? For untold thousands of years they were the kings of this continent, and where would the plains grizzlies have found these trees on the bald-headed prairies?

It is a fact that an adult grizzly bear's claws are not shaped for climbing, and while they have scurried up trees after people, they mainly do it by wrapping their paws around the trees or above branches.

In all our confrontations with grizzly bears they never attempted to send their cubs up trees. They always took them with them when they left a carcass and woe to the person who tried to stop them.

Another point I would like to make is that if I was stationary and the grizzlies stumbled onto me in the mountains, they seemed to leave without getting excited to any degree. But if I walked into them, the mother appeared instantly ready to do battle.

Professor Herrero makes it plain not to play dead in the case of a male black bear attack. He points out that this is a predatory attack so one must fight or escape. He is exactly right and I ask people to realize that these bears are not coming to play a game of checkers. They will kill and eat you, and there are countless examples around to prove this statement. I know of a few from my own experiences and acquaintances.

Another example of the unpredictability of bears is shown in the following—a canoe trip down the Hulahula River in the Arctic National Wildlife Refuge. During their 2005 canoe trip, Rich and Kathy Huffman had followed procedure to the letter. They had eaten a long distance from their tent camp, and they had all their food in bear-proof containers. Yet they were attacked in their tent, killed and partly eaten before Rich had a chance to use his firearm. The area guide found their remains and was chased quite a distance downriver before the bear got tangled up with a boulder and aborted the chase.

This guide begged to differ when he suggested that bear-proof containers should not be used. He deliberately leaves some food out and covers it with pots and pans. That way the bear wakes him up and gives him the chance to defend both himself and the others he is charged with protecting.

Herrero's statement that, "Because bears in the northern environment are more food-stressed plays a large part in their being more dangerous than their southern cousins," rings true. The long winters play a huge part in that, with late frosts often playing havoc with the berry crops on which the bears are so dependent. Some years there is such a huckleberry crop in Central BC that it could feed a million bears; other years they are almost nonexistent.

As to what caused the increase in attacks on humans in Yellowstone Park, I believe the increase in bear numbers had a direct bearing on it. Grizzly numbers had increased from 136 bears in 1975 to 602 by 2010. As well, throughout the lower 48 states, the numbers have bounced back from about 550 in 1973, to 1,700 today. This number has met all the population goals that had been set by the Grizzly Bear Recovery Program.

Chris Servheen also added a rather pertinent point, "Grizzlies food-switch; they have the ability to eat things when they're available and then go to something else when they are not. If you wanted to design an animal that would be optimally resilient to global warming, it would be omnivorous, an animal that lives in a wide variety of elevations and aspects, and one that is very adept at food-switching. The animal you designed would look a lot like a grizzly bear."

Up until this point the debating had remained rather quiet, but when the two human bodies were partly eaten by these bears, things really began heating up. Some officials want the hunting season opened, while others are vehemently against it. As well, tremendous pressure has been exerted by ranchers and hunters to open a season and teach the bears to fear man once again. One of the people attendant at a meeting suggested that if pushed, the hunters and ranchers would resort to "Shoot, shovel and shut up."

This opened another can of worms and caused a fierce debate as to whether hunting would teach the bears anything.

Scott Talbott of Wyoming Game and Fish, along with Harv Forsgren of the U.S. Forest Service claimed that sport hunting would help the grizzly bear recovery by reducing human-bear conflicts. They also claimed that their conclusions were based on the best available science and on public opinion.

On the opposing side, George Wuerthner countered by stating that, "Sport hunting of bears is an indiscriminate activity, so it would not target animals involved in conflicts. Also, hunted bears cannot learn to be wary of people or avoid attractants because they are dead by definition, and dead bears can't learn."

Contrary to what many believe, hunting takes a lot of the aggression out of them. Having been there and done that, I know for a fact that when wandering grizzlies find another grizzly lying dead, with human scent around it, they get the message loud and clear. When we hunted grizzlies around the Grizzly Bear Mountain area, we almost never saw boar grizzlies out in the open during the day. Sometimes we would see them just after daybreak, but they always quit feeding and moved into cover shortly thereafter. Again, we would sometimes see them on an adjacent ridge just before dark, when we didn't have time to get to them. The few times we did see them out in the open during the day there were usually explanations or other grizzlies associated with it.

One afternoon a friend named Marlin Priebe and I watched a sow grizzly as she grazed a short distance below timberline. It was an extremely hot afternoon in August, and that heat forced a boar grizzly to emerge from a subalpine clump of trees. It walked to a spring that had cut a trough out of the mountain, looked it over and then slid down in. It rolled over until its feet were sticking straight up in the air and just stayed there with the cool water running around its body. We both agreed that the reason the boar felt so secure was because the sow was right below him, to warn him of approaching danger.

Many times I noticed how grizzlies gained a feeling of security and were less secretive when other grizzlies were around.

But their secretive nature changed considerably after we stopped hunting them for about eight or ten years, because then these boars were out feeding in the open at midday. They do put things together and figure them out.

Here is another example: for many years we hunted the railroad grade in the spring when there were countless moose carcasses strewn along the grade. Often we walked about five miles in the dark, and heard the bears go crashing through the woods on our approach. In those many encounters with grizzlies, we never had a bear even bluff charge us. Yet there were two and possibly three men killed by grizzlies in that general area when they stumbled into a grizzly on a moose carcass out in the woods. I firmly believe the bears figured these moose belonged to a big, noisy creature that came along every day. The bears would move back into cover until the trains passed and then return to their feasts. They somehow seemed to sense that these carcasses did not belong to them and for that reason were far less aggressive. I truly believe that if we had blundered into these carcasses in the woods, we would have been mauled or killed.

The only person who got mauled along the railroad in that area was Heller Hreczka. He was walking the railroad in dull moonlight and was not making any noise. He wandered right between a mother and cub grizzly that were feeding on a train-killed domestic cow, at which point she attacked and mauled him. Heller survived with many scars to show for the one-sided fight.

What is happening in Yellowstone has already taken place countless times throughout history. When bear populations explode, they become more aggressive and that is a given. For instance, during the first 40-some years I spent around this mountain, I never noticed a grizzly chasing another grizzly, but during the last 10 years I spent up there this became a common event, which we managed to capture on film. With the increase in numbers came a corresponding increase in aggressive behaviour.

I stress the point that when we were hunting these bears every year, they became ghostlike. Now with very limited hunting and declining wolf numbers in some areas, the increasing grizzly numbers in parts of BC have made them extremely aggressive.

Lloyd Vandermark of McBride, BC, described one of his adventures up the Muskwa River in northern BC in 2005. He shot an elk late in the day and returned to the scene the following morning with two friends to get the meat. Before they got close, they could see it had been dragged for a short distance, so they went in carefully. A grizzly had been at work and had only eaten a little, indicating the bear had just recently found it. It was fairly open in the area, so Lloyd stood guard while the others finished dressing out the animal. Then they packed the quarters about a third of a mile away where they stashed them up above the ground as best they could arrange it. The following day they returned to pack the meat back to camp and found the bear had packed it all away. It was also apparent the bear had tracked them and found it, so this begs the question of what would have happened if they had taken the meat back to their camp.

Lloyd also assured me that several other hunters have had the same experience in that area. Once you have an animal down, the greatest possible care is the order of the day.

I'm thinking of the family that raised a black bear cub in my hometown of Penny, BC, because its mother had been killed by a

Jack and Clarence with a big grizzly that Clarence shot in 1966.

train. One day the children were playing when they started screaming in fun, as children often do. This caused the excited bear to attack one of the children. The child survived, but the bear had to be destroyed.

A habituated bear is a dead bear unless it is being held in captivity or, as in Charlie Russell's case, behind an electric fence.

Because this is a life and death issue concerning our future offspring, I need to ask a question here—if we can live in peace with these bears, then why did Charlie Russell take an electric fence to Kamchatka? Perhaps he did not want to end up like Michio Hoshino, the photographer attacked and eaten outside an electric fence in that general area.

I repeat my belief that bears should stay *wild*, for their own sake and for the safety of humans.

Throughout the years, an astounding amount of wildlife has been killed along our nation's highways and railways. Somehow it was accepted as the cost of doing business, but things are slowly changing.

Giant steps have been taken in an effort to prevent wildlife deaths by vehicles in Banff National Park, where wildlife crossing structures have been installed. After the Trans-Canada Highway was upgraded to a four-lane divided highway in the 1980s, vehicle-wildlife accidents became commonplace. When wildlife crossings were constructed and the highway fenced in order to guide wildlife toward the crossings, vehicle accidents dropped considerably. The idea caught on, and today there are 24 underpasses and 4 overpasses in that area. As well, more are being constructed near Lake Louise. Since the installation of these crossings, over 200,000 wildlife crossings have been recorded, and wildlife fatalities have dropped by more than 80 percent.

As hard as it may be to believe, during the summer about 25,000 vehicles use this highway every day, which means a vehicle passes every two to three seconds. It seems almost unbelievable that an animal could make it across one lane, never mind four lanes of the highway, without getting hit.

Another point that should be made is this: when animals cannot gain access to the roadsides, they cannot be enticed to hang around by thoughtless tourists offering food. Therefore, fewer vehicle-animal accidents. Since these underpasses have been proven a success, why not try the same ideas along some of the railways, especially in high-density game areas? As shown by these experiences along the Banff highway, it takes time for the wildlife to feel comfortable using them, but once they do, they teach their young and as time passes they will be used more and more.

Up until now, the railroads have had a free pass and have not had to answer for the slaughter of wildlife that has gone on for decades. Sometimes the slaughter was almost beyond comprehension.

During a heavy snowfall winter in the late 1960s, Clarence

and I counted 148 moose carcasses in 24 miles of railway grade. In some natural crossing areas we found four or five carcasses touching each other. On another occasion over half of a mountain caribou herd was wiped out in the Longworth area of the CNR's Fraser Subdivision. I'm not faulting the railroads, for in some instances they slowed the trains and drove the moose for miles before they gave up and ran them down. Understandably, the moose would refuse to get off the grade with shoulder-deep snow to flounder in. Although well meaning, this driving moose for miles in cold weather was doomed to failure, for as we noticed, these animals got pneumonia and died later anyway.

But that was then and this is now; surely we have to ask ourselves if this slaughter must go on forever.

Underpasses would be so much easier to construct along the narrow railroad grade when compared to a two- or four-lane highway. But problems could arise during winters with heavy snowfall. If the snowplows dumped large amounts of snow along their entrances and exits, the wildlife could not gain access. This means snow-sheds would have to be erected on both sides of the grades to prevent this buildup of snow. From time to time the railroads have to replace old culverts. This would be the natural place to put these underpasses, by having the stream and the walkway go side by side. Animals follow streams, so why not give it a try? I believe these streams would give the animals an added sense of security.

I am not advocating the use of the low page-wire fences that were used back when I was a lad, because in winters with deep snow conditions the moose frequently got tangled up in them and hung there with broken legs. But in natural crossing areas these underpasses would definitely help, and the game would learn to use them over time.

Hunter with second-largest stone sheep. Photo Dave Wiens.

Timber wolf. Photo Dusty Palmer.

Photo Dusty Palmer.

Photo above and below: Young timber wolves with mom. Steve Schwartz.

A herd of caribou grazing on the mountainside. Photo Dusty Palmer.

Photo above: Three majestic caribou. Photographer unknown.
Photo below: Mule deer buck. Leon Lorenz.

Photo above: Three deer posing for the camera. Steve Schwartz.
Photo below: Bull moose. Leon Lorenz.

Photo above: A grizzly on Torpy River with a salmon breakfast. Leon Lorenz.
Photo below: A charging grizzly bear. Dusty Palmer.

Photo above : Grizzlies fishing on Torpy River. Leon Lorenz.
Photo below: A black bear family foraging. Steve Schwartz.

Mountain meadow in the McBride area. Photo Leon Lorenz.

Photo above: Ruffled grouse. Leon Lorenz.
Photo below: Marten. Leon Lorenz.

Photo above: A young great horned owl. Leon Lorenz
Photo below: A cougar in the Robson Valley. Leon Lorenz.

Bald eagle. Photo Dusty Palmer.

Photo Dusty Palmer.

PART TWO

ADVENTURES IN THE WILDERNESS

To be a guide in a rugged mountain setting is to experience the ultimate sense of freedom. Every day is a new adventure where you get to meet nature on its own terms. Small wonder so many guides and outfitters love their way of life so dearly.

Most of them say they would do it again without a second's consideration. Some even say they would do it without pay if they could afford to.

I know a guide named Bill Eckert who left a job that paid $200 a day to go guiding for the sum of $20 a day. When I queried him about the logic of his decision, he replied, "Without a doubt the years I spent guiding were the best years of my life."

Over the last 50 years I have spent many hours listening to stories of guiding adventures in the remotest parts of BC. Many of of these guides state that their lives have been spent in what can best be described as paradise.

One guide summed up his life experiences by saying, "Even though I have had to deal with a few oddballs, others have made it all worthwhile by leaving tips and other gifts that showed their appreciation."

Here's an example of a hunter's appreciation: a guide in the area east of Prince George, BC, lucked out and got his American hunter a record-sized grizzly and a monster moose, and all on the same hunt. When they arrived back at base, the hunter squared up

Trail Camp. Photo Dave Wiens.

for the trip and then handed the guide a letter containing $5,000. This was about 50 years ago and represented a quarter year's wages at that time. As if that wasn't enough, he spread the word around and gave the outfitter a fortune worth of free advertising.

Another guide stated, "Adventure, that's what it has been; almost 40 years of adventures and I made a decent living as well." Another one offered, "I worked at many different jobs before I got into guiding. I found some of those jobs boring beyond words. One thing I can say is that this life has always been interesting, and always exciting; I have never felt bored because there is always something that needs doing, such as tending to horses, supplying camps, cutting trails, or the most rewarding of all, dressing out trophies for hunters who can't hide their satisfaction and appreciation."

One thing is for certain, climbing around the mountains certainly keeps one in top physical condition. I know from experience that carrying heavy packs up steep mountains does not lead to obesity. As well, there is a special bond that develops between hunters and guides that often lasts a lifetime. They share some of life's greatest moments together in remote areas where they are forced to depend on each other, and this creates a bond that never dies.

Larry Whitesitt

Since I wrote the book *Wild & Free,* about Frank Cooke guiding in the Kechika Mountains, I have had the opportunity to talk with bush pilot Larry Whitesitt. Larry flew Beaver aircraft out of Watson Lake during the 1970s, and authored the books *Flight of the Red Beaver* and *Northern Flight of Dreams.* Larry is now retired and living in Washington State.

When we got to discussing his years of bush flying, he told me an interesting story that illustrates that despite the beauty and excitement of living in the wilderness, it's not all sunshine and roses out there in the mountains. There are stresses that have built up to the point where they exploded, such as the problems that have occurred between guides and resident hunters. From what I understand, thankfully this is mostly a thing of the past.

One fall about 50 years ago he flew a resident hunter into a wilderness lake for a Stone's sheep hunt, with orders to pick him up in two weeks' time. After Larry flew away, the hunter proceeded to put up his tent and camp right beside the trail that the guides had cut to access the mountain top.

Two weeks later, when Larry returned to the pickup spot, he found the hunter still sitting in his camp, white-faced and shaken. Larry inquired and learned that the hunter had never left his camp. After he settled down, the hunter informed Larry that just after he set up his campsite, a local guide walked up to him with a handgun pointed at his chest and told him that if he was found hunting on the mountain he could expect to have his f***ing head blown off. The hunter was only too happy to see the last of that area and was flown out without a hunt. Such was the situation with the guides cutting the trails, only to find the resident hunters taking advantage of their efforts.

Dave Wiens

Other guides learned to work with the resident hunters and it worked out best for all. One such outfitter was Dave Wiens, who owned the guiding area east of Skook's ranch at Terminus Mountain.

Here is Dave's story.

"I was born in '51 in southern Alberta and then my family moved to the town of Ryley. I thought it was wonderful coming from a town and moving to a farm. It was tough being in grade four at that time because the peer pressure was awful. I finally had to fight the toughest guy in the class. I managed to get him in a choke hold and held him until he was turning purple. I asked him if he had enough and he made it plain that he had. I never had any trouble in school after that.

"I grew up on a dairy farm, where we had mixed grains, hogs and chickens—we had it all. We grew up learning how to work. It was nothing but work. One day I asked my dad to give me a dollar a day to milk all 35 cows, but he wouldn't because he was already providing for all my needs.

"I met my future wife, Ellie, who lived in the next town and went to the church we attended. The funny thing was that when Mom and Dad saw her as a five-year-old they said, 'There is Dave's wife!' They had her picked out long before I did. She is the only girl I ever dated. We got married young. I think I was 20 and she was 19.

"I was working in Edmonton at that time. All the young people were going to the city to work, so I went too. It didn't take long for us to realize that the city was not for us, so we came back and bought my grandfather's farm at Ryley for $45,000. I got three quarter-sections of land, and the best part of all, Alberta Farm Development Corporation gave me full backing for the land. All I had to do was provide them with a management plan and my dad secured it with one quarter-section of land. They gave me a 100 percent loan. The bank was good to me, because they gave me a $25,000 operating loan and I was in business. I raised hogs. I had 60 sows, so we had pigs dropping every three days. When the pigs got a disease, we had to get out of that business completely. At that time, we were using Dad's equipment and working back and forth helping each other out, and then we started buying our own equipment. That was in 1972.

"To top it off, as if the pig disease wasn't bad enough, we were hailed out three out of five years. The first year I didn't have any insurance, but I bought some after that just to cover expenses. The next year I bought more insurance, up to $100 per acre and we got 100 percent hailed out. Those were the years when there was no quota for selling grain so we got 100 percent paid out. It turned out that it was kind of a blessing to get hailed out. We still managed to get 10 bushels per acre so it was a good deal. Anyway, the last year I farmed it rained so much that we couldn't pull the combine through the fields because we were leaving three-foot ruts. I finally decided that there must be something easier than this so we sold out. My wife and I and my cousin began looking for land up in the Peace River country because land had not gone up in price there yet.

"We were looking for land when we ran into a realtor who had a hunting area for sale in BC I asked him to explain because I had no idea what a hunting area was. So he showed us pictures and I said, 'That just can't be. How can anyone make a living going out hunting?' It seemed just too good to be true, but we decided to look into it. It was by Mile 747 on the Alaska Highway. The business was not doing well, but four of us decided to give it a shot. One guy had some guiding experience and my cousin was going to learn to fly, which we needed because some of the areas were fly-in jobs. One of the other guys seemed to know something about horses, so I was prepared to have a go at it with them."

I queried Dave about the wisdom of putting their money into something they knew nothing about, adding that it was the main reason people went broke in business.

"Yes, but the deal didn't pan out, so in 1979 we phoned the Game Department in Fort St. John and talked to a biologist named John Elliot, and asked if he knew of any guiding areas for sale. He told us of a couple guiding areas for sale but stressed that there was one at Toad River and said it was probably the best guiding area in BC.

"The owner was Bob Kjos, who had been guiding there since 1966. He wanted over half a million bucks for it, and he invited us to come on up and have a look. He also added that he was willing to finance us. So the four of us went up and convinced him to sell it to us. At that time it was the most expensive guiding territory in BC. We convinced Bob to kind of run it for two years until we could get the hang of it. He would do the flying, supply the guides and teach us the ropes. Bob agreed and that was enough to give us a chance. I stayed at the ranch the first year and learned all I could about the operation, as the ranch went with the guiding area. So we each put a deposit down of $50,000 and he financed the rest at 12 percent over 10 years.

Dave in Super Cub at Cabin Creek airstrip. Photo Dave Wiens.

"As it turned out, before the ink was dry on the deal, one of the fellows backed out. He decided it was not going to work. He was the one with all the experience, which meant we had to come up with his share of the deposit, so it came out of the money on hand. This really put us behind the eight-ball. Anyway, we got the season kind of rolling, and we were already into the season one month when the second partner informed us that he hadn't sold his property, so he didn't have the money either. As he had nothing in it, I gave him my truck and he walked away from the deal. This meant we had to come up with $75,000 each. We had to finance that part, which we did over three years. We gave Bob back the airplane that we had purchased, and that covered part of the payment. This really left us in a bind. Our revenue was $200,000 but our payments were $100,000. This went on for three years. We were living off our child allowance; that's all we had to live on. The rest all went into the business and our efforts to keep things moving.

"A bit of luck came our way when we got a record-book Stone's sheep. We won an award from the North American Sheep Foundation for the #1 sheep. This put us on the map as far as trophy hunting. This meant we were able to raise our prices and book up solid. Those were the years when oil was going good so we had a lot of hunters from Texas. At least half our hunters came from Texas.

"Bob had his crew there and we were working for them. Imagine how humiliating that was—we were the owners and we were taking orders. Bob had me out as a wrangler, learning the trade, so of course he had to be the boss. I had no prior horse experience so I had no choice; I had to start there. By the end of the season the crew told me I was a good man, and that I knew my business. After that I started guiding and I guided for six straight years. Then in 1985 my cousin and I decided it was time to part our ways. So I named a price and told him he could buy me out or I would buy him out. He decided to sell and I found another partner in Calgary. His name was Archie Nesbitt and he was a famous bow hunter who had hunted all over the world. Anyway I guided him on a hunt and he became my partner. He stayed in Calgary and I ran the business. We had a fabulous partnership for 20 years. By 1987 we finally got

65 percent ownership of the business. That's when the outfit really took off and flourished.

"The first year we were on our own we won #1, #2 and #4 sheep. That really put us on the map, and that's when prices went up in a hurry. Then we kept building up the business, especially our camps, which were in dire need of upgrading. We built numerous cabins, airstrips, tent frames for our camp-out sites and trail systems. We also built up the ranch including a hangar for the airplane and a walk-in meat cooler. In 1985 I got my flying licence; it just took me 30 hours. The next year, 1987, I went back and got my commercial licence and I did all the flying after that until I sold it in 2005."

Dave's adventures in the air

"The first year I marked out a strip on the runway at the ranch 10 feet wide by 500 feet long. I practised over and over putting the plane down in that area even with a cross-wind. When I got that down pat I knew I could land on a mountain strip. I started out with the best strips and by the end of that year I had landed on all of them. Also that first year, with 50 hours of flying time, I started flying my clients in and out of those mountain strips. Some of those runways were so bad that I wouldn't fly in there today. It is amazing that I didn't bite the dust during those years. When you're flying, you don't know your limits until you've reached those limits. I had a Super Cub at that time. I bought it to do my training and it felt so natural I decide to keep it. I managed to solo in one hour; it just seemed to fit me. Once I got in the Super Cub it seemed so natural that it almost flew itself. I flew into one mountain strip that was only 300 feet long, and then there was a drop of another 300 feet to where it came out above a lake. We put a little rise at the end so it would give a lift if the plane wasn't in the air yet. It was soft sand so very hard to manoeuvre in.

"Well, I survived it and that same year a hunter had broken his rifle so I went back to get his gun. The next day I was flying it back in to the strip and the clouds looked really weird. They kept growing larger and larger as I flew along. It was calm so I flew all the way to Sheep Creek Camp, dropped off the gun and stayed only about five minutes. I knew I had to get out of there because it was closing in. So I took off, and lo and behold, I couldn't get out of the valley; it was socked in. I flew as high as I could and tried to radio Fort Nelson to let them know I was going to stay at the camp, but I couldn't get through on the radio. I waited until I knew the CP Air flight was in the air and I tried to radio them to pass the message along, but I didn't reach them either. So I was stuck in there for three days with rain and fog blanketing the area. After three days like that, the weather turned to snow and it turned out that I was stuck for five days. Ellie knew where I had gone, but not what had happened. Nobody could fly because of the weather, but they did send a ground party out. Then, because of the weather, they got lost. By the time they got to camp, I had flown out. But before I flew out, a neighbouring guide named Gary Vince, who was very experienced in mountain flying, managed to fly in by following the creek. I asked him if I could fly out and he told me to stay put. He flew out and told my wife that I was okay. As it turned out, the search party had already left so they were out there in the woods on their own.

"Some of the ice melted off the plane and the rest we got off by pouring hot water over it. Well, I survived that episode but there was always more. That was the first year, but the next year with my commercial licence I started flying full-time. I had to learn how to fly in severe weather just to get the job done. There were many occasions where we were pushing the point of safety, but it went with the job. I recall the time I went to visit Ross Peck, the neighbouring outfitter to the south of me. It was beautiful weather so I thought I would wait until evening to fly in and check my Sheep Creek hunting camp. The runway in there was short and so I wanted calm air for the trip. After supper I took off from Ross's camp and found a massive storm brewing. This made me change my mind, so I decided to head for home.

"In nothing flat, the clouds were everywhere and they were green and purple, with lightning flashing all around me. I considered going back to Ross's camp, but when I looked behind me there was nothing but massive clouds everywhere. I kept going and had three choices: Cabin Creek runway, or a little strip we had beside the highway, or I could fly into my Tetsa camp. I flew over Cabin Creek, but it was so rough there was not a chance I could land. I continued along with my eyes almost closed because the lightning was flashing continually. All at once I got flipped right upside down and the plane was stressed so much that both my doors came open—it felt like I had lost half my plane. I got the plane right side up again and got the doors closed and was flying toward the highway, but when I got there I couldn't see the highway because it was raining so hard. If I had tried to land there I may have run right into a vehicle. So I looked up the valley and thought that my Tetsa camp was my last chance. I had to land there. My worry was that horses may be on the runway as they often were. As I came in, I estimated that I had a 40- to 50-mile-per-hour tailwind. There was no possibility that I could turn around in that valley; I was committed to land. My salvation that day was that the runway was uphill and I managed to get stopped.

"The crew came out with their laundry and things, thinking I had just made a routine stop, but I wasn't going anywhere. Instead, they had to help me get the plane turned around and tied down in the continuous wind.

"On another occasion I was flying a client into our Tetsa camp when I got into a bad situation. I had already flown his wife in, and it started raining so hard I could not see out the windshield. I could not turn around in that narrow valley with the strong wind, so I was committed to land. I had no choice but to land looking out only my side window. Had there been horses on the runway, who knows what would have happened. To make matters worse, the rain was coming through the windshield. It wasn't sealed that well, so everything was soaked. Anyway, it cleared a bit later so I took off and flew home.

"I remember an accident I had when I landed downwind— that was with the L19. It was a beautiful evening and I was flying a heavy load into the upper Tetsa camp. We had built a runway there

Dave's ace assistant, Red Cloud, with two fine moose. Photo Dave Wiens.

about 700 feet long that was on a pretty good slope. But you had to land uphill, or you would have trouble getting stopped. I was coming in with a heavy load, about 800 pounds and the wind was blowing hard up the valley. This meant I had to land downhill. I came in downhill, and just as I was flared out and almost at stall speed, a gust of wind hit me from behind and just pushed me down the runway. There I was skidding down the runway and unable to stop. When I reached the end of the runway, I hit this big hump, so up and over I went, right into a big clump of willows. I got out and looked things over, and though the plane looked alright, I had torn the right brake line off. This meant I had no right brake, and that's the one you need the most because it acts as a counter-torque. I was at the wrong end of the runway with a big load, so what to do? I ran to the camp and luckily there was an axe there. I cut all the willows around the plane, and although there were a few dents in the plane, the prop looked okay. It wasn't bent, just rather green from chopping willows. Well, I unloaded the plane and then used a big rock, which I placed in behind one wheel, and then grabbed the tail and leveraged it around. I then blocked the other wheel and leveraged it around until I got the plane back on the runway. I reloaded the stuff and taxied the plane back to the camp at the other end of the strip, and then I had to pack all the supplies into the cabin.

"By the time I finished, I was wasted and it was getting dark. I set the plane up at an angle so that I wouldn't need the right brake until I could control the plane with the tail rudder, and took off downhill with my lights on. It was dark by then but once I got up I could see well enough to continue on. I radioed my wife and told her to clear the deer and the elk off the runway, and then to position the truck with the lights shining along the runway. She did and I came in right over the truck and made a successful landing. The next day I repaired the brake line and got it ready to go again. By that time the guiding was going successfully, as we had experienced guides and great clientele."

Dave could see I was interested so I didn't have to beg him to continue.

"There was also the time I flew into Ram Mountain Camp. I had a big load going in there and just as I landed I heard a big *pop* and I could hear this thundering in the back of the plane. What happened was the tail spring broke and my tail wheel was flopping back there against the airplane. So we unloaded the plane, took the wheel off and put it inside. I went to the end of the runway, gave it full power and held the brakes on until the tail lifted, then I took off without putting any weight on the back of the plane. I took off and radioed Fort Nelson that I was coming in without a tail-wheel. I wanted to land on the grass but they wanted me to land as far away from everything as possible. They asked if I wanted the fire trucks and ambulance but I told them it was not necessary. I kept the power and full flaps on and used the brakes to slow down. Then I put the tail down, and the brakes were some hot by the time I got stopped. I broke a few tail springs because of heavy loads and running into bumps. They get stressed and break with time. I tried building my own with truck springs but they broke anyway.

"My L19 had 250 horses, so that's a lot of get-up-and-go. It would get off in 190 feet. Generally I could be off in 500 feet with a full load. If it came off the ground, it would fly."

I asked Dave to deal with a rumour I had heard about when he tipped the plane on its nose, just to prove he was human.

"Yes, I was done flying for the day in the mountains and was coming home. I had nothing in the back because I had taken everything including the seats out to make room for the big load I had hauled. I landed and turned around at the end of the runway and suddenly the tail started lifting up. It shocked me so I pulled the power off. That was a mistake; I should have applied power instead. When I took the power off, the tail kept coming up and up, right over on the nose. The prop was still turning, so it struck the ground and stayed there. I had to crawl down to the ground from that position.

"I obviously had a prop strike, so there was a possibility that it damaged the crank. I taxied back to the hangar and luckily we had a hunter there who was an engineer; I think he was from Rolls Royce. He was good with metal properties and he said, 'You know, I don't think this is that bad; I think we can straighten it.' So just with clamps and blocks, using it for leverage, we straightened that prop right out. Just a cold stretch and it looked fine. One blade was undamaged and I had another prop so we compared them and got it exactly the same. Then I started it up and took it for a spin and it was smoother than it had ever been, so I kept flying it until the end of the season.

"I couldn't afford to pull the engine right then so I just sent the prop in after the hunting season to get it overhauled and told them to x-ray it, which they did. They said it was fine. I asked them to x-ray it again because it had a strike. They did, and said it was good to go. So I flew it for a couple years and then one day I was flying along at about 6,000 feet with a full load and suddenly my engine quit as if I had turned the key off. No vibration, no coughing, nothing. Then I plainly heard a voice in the plane that said, 'It's not your time yet.' I looked out the windshield and there was the Alaska Highway and it was the only long straight stretch in that area. On top of that, there was not one vehicle in sight. I had to land it downhill, and it seemed a lot steeper than I remembered from driving it. I had a hard time stopping it and when I did, I was just a matter of feet from a bridge that would have torn the wings off the plane. There was a turn-out close by so I was relieved to get the plane off the road. I had a satellite phone with me so I called my wife, told her the story, and asked her to come and get me. I also called and ordered another engine and told the mechanic that I needed an overhaul. I think I was just about timed out on the engine so it needed an overhaul anyway.

"It turned out that a gear that runs the magneto had come off, and there was a chance that it had been damaged when I tipped the plane and had that prop strike. Even though it ran for several years, that strike may have had something to do with it."

I allowed that he had pushed his luck that day, especially being fully loaded. I also asked if that engine failure discouraged him from flying into those mountain passes.

"No, because those words I heard in the plane that day gave me the courage to keep flying. Actually one of my worst scares happened a few years before that last incident when we had one of those bad weather spells, which we got every year. It was one of those 10-day periods where you get rain, fog and snow. Well, this spell had already been going on for 10 days and I knew the camps were out of food. I knew they needed supplies so I started to push it a bit. I managed to service all but this one camp, and it was a tough ride out of there for the guides to get supplies. In fact, it was a seven-hour ride just to get out of there. So I flew up the valley and there was just enough ceiling to get the plane through a pass. There were four passes I had to get through, so I poked through the second pass and there was a V, or opening, to let me through again. I worked my way through and managed to get into the camp, where I delivered the groceries and picked up the meat and garbage to go out again. I took off and got through the first two passes only to find the third pass socked in.

"So there I was, forced to circle around with only a meadow below me that was too small to land in. I flew as slow as possible, between 60 and 70 mph, and had to be sure to keep the trail below in reference, because if I lost my sense of direction I was finished. I knew what elevation I needed to clear the pass—exactly 3,200 feet. I was at 3,100 feet, so I lined up with the trail and climbed just over the trees into the fog. I could barely make out the trees below me so I followed through just above them and dropped until I broke into the clear again. I managed to get out of that one, but I must have lost a year of my life right there. I was terrified, and I kept thinking this is so crazy. That was a bad spot, and I know of other planes that got lost in there and ended up glued to the hills."

I agreed that he really pushed the envelope that time, adding that many bush pilots got killed because of fog, and that included some of the best. I reminded him that Russ Baker almost got it when he was flying a married couple into the mountains. They got into a sucker hole when the pass ahead of him closed in, so they got turned around and found the pass behind them had closed in tight as well. They circled in a valley for one hour and luckily one pass opened up and allowed them to escape what would have been a certain death sentence.

"I can relate to what they went through," Dave said. "It's an exciting and rewarding life to fly like that, but it is certainly hard on the nerves at times. One day I had to fly into one of our camps and the cloud cover was down to about 500 feet. Where I had to land was on the other side of the pass, or the other side of Summit Lake. I thought I could see some light on the other side of the pass so I took off, while Ellie drove the clients to an airstrip the other side of the pass. I intended to shuttle them to our hunting camp from there. I took off and sure enough I could see a hole with the sun shining brightly through it. So I finished moving everything to the camp and was on my way home with a client on board while Ellie had the client's wife in the truck. When I got through the pass, everything was a sea of fog. I radioed my daughter at the ranch and asked how the weather looked there. She told me it was about the same as when I left, so I knew there was visibility down under the fog. I flew along until I was just above the Racing River, not far from home, and knew exactly where I was by the mountain peaks sticking up out of the fog. There was just a layer of about 1,000 feet of fog. I had the option of going up the valley and trying to get under the fog, as I had done before, but I also knew I was only five miles from home. As well, I could see the ground, so I slowed down, gave it a notch of flap, and circled my way down into this hole in the fog. These holes are appropriately called 'sucker holes' because a pilot may not come out of them alive.

"When I got near the bottom, there was fog all around me. I couldn't climb back up because there were mountains all around me. I knew if I followed the river I could reach my neighbour's ranch and make an emergency landing in his fields, so I followed the river about four feet above the water, and visibility of only 100 feet. My main worry was that I had to fly over or under a bridge before I got there. There were also leaning trees sticking out into the river and I had to dodge them. I called Ellie, who was on the road beside me, and asked, 'Ellie, can you see anything? Because I can't.'

"She answered, 'No, I'm in fog!'"

"Audrey came on from the ranch and stated it was still the same as before. By that time I was so tensed up that I could hardly move. I gave it more power and speeded up and when I saw the bridge, I managed to climb over it. At the same time, I saw the yellow line shine through so I followed the highway. On one side was a series of cliffs and on the other side tall trees. I was about 80 to 100 feet above the ground and it was getting harder and harder to see. What I didn't realize was that my windshield was fogging up because of the heavy moisture. I was looking out my side window and jumping over tall trees and I was so tense it was hardly bearable. It continued like that for about three miles and then I could see some light ahead. That was when I realized my windshield was all fogged in. I cleaned it off and finally made it home. After I landed and parked the plane, I turned to my client and said, 'I'm really sorry!'

"He answered, 'For what?'

"Rather surprised, I told him, 'Well, things weren't very safe.'

"He didn't have a clue that we had been in great danger, and maybe it was a blessing that he didn't know, because I sure didn't need a panicked person in the plane to distract me. Well when I got out of the plane I could hardly walk because of the tension."

I pointed out to Dave that from the many stories I had read about bush pilots, sucker holes were one of their greatest enemies and many never came out of situations like that. It was truly a case of being totally committed.

Dave answered, "That was a perfect example of a sucker hole; by the time you realize you are in trouble there is no way out. All the indications I had to go on were that it was good when it wasn't. You have to remember that and make sure you never try it again. And that is exactly right—I was totally committed. The only choices I had were to crash into the Racing River with its big boulders, which would have completely destroyed the plane, or else try to make it home.

"We did everything we could think of to make things safe. In the mountains we always improved on the airstrips. We pulled out all the big rocks and made them as safe as possible.

"I have another airplane story and this is not my own story.

"Two men from Germany were flying around the world in a Mooney airplane. They had found out about our place through the tourism industry so they wanted to land and film it. The plane was following the highway up to Alaska and going across Canada. They had a film crew stationed at the ranch with an interpreter, so I asked him, 'What is a Mooney?' I had no idea at that time. He explained it was a small, high-performance plane. He also said he felt sure that there was enough room to put it down on our runway.

"They phoned when they left Fort Nelson, which is about an hour away. But the weather had worsened because a thunderstorm had just gone through. The air currents were a little weird and the wind had switched. I had hoped that these guys were at least half smart and knew what they are doing, but at the same time I had a bad feeling inside. I had told them that I would place my plane beside the runway and point it in the direction they were to land, and according to the plan, their crew was to film the landing. As they came along, the interpreter was talking to them on my airplane radio. I told him to tell them to be sure to land going west. Well, they came roaring into the valley and I thought they were going to just take a look at things. Instead, he dropped his wheels as though he was going to land at the wrong end, with a tailwind. I ran out into the middle of the runway and began waving him up with both arms. I was also shouting but of course they couldn't hear me. Besides, the film crew was telling me to be quiet. I shouted, 'He can't land! He's going to crash!'

"The pilot kept coming down until he was about two feet off the runway and he was floating with this tailwind. And this is a hot little airplane; he was going a hundred miles an hour on approach, and it looked as though he intended to land.

"My runway was only 1,500 feet long and he needed all of it in good conditions. So by the time he was halfway down the runway, he hadn't touched the ground yet. By then I was thinking, 'He's done. I know he's done, but how can he be so stupid?'

"By then he gave it power to go around, but the airplane wasn't responding. It sounded like the engine was missing. When it went by us, it wasn't six feet off the ground and it was heading into a spring cut, with tall trees on both sides and a tailwind pushing the plane. He tried to climb out of it but the mountain was steeper than his climb so he started clipping trees with his wings. Suddenly the airplane did a 360-degree turn and went right into the mountain.

"The people filming were so horrified they couldn't even speak. I started running toward the house and heard a huge explosion, so I knew they were both dead. I told my daughter to phone Ken, the chopper pilot, and tell him to get here quickly for an emergency medivac for two people. As well, she phoned the ambulance in Toad River to come at once. Of course the ambulance people thought it was me that crashed.

"My wife, another guy and I headed to the crash site with a spade because we knew the bush was dry and there would be a fire. When we got to the plane, flames were pouring out of the cockpit because fuel drums and oxygen tanks were going up. I got a look inside the plane and there was nobody in there; I thought maybe they had fallen out. We walked around the plane and found a trail of fire leading away from the plane. We followed it and found the two men. Before the plane blew up, they had gotten out.

"They were terribly burned. One man couldn't see; his eyes, nose and ears were gone. All that was left was this burnt lump of flesh. The other guy was badly burnt as well. I told Ellie to stay with them because she was an ambulance attendant. The other guy and I put the fire out so it wouldn't spread and cause a big forest fire. Then I ran down to meet the ambulance crew and get some clean sheets and water and things. The ambulance crew came back with us and we finally managed to get them out of there. By that time the helicopter arrived so one of them went by air and the other by ambulance.

"The end result was that one guy lived for three weeks and the other was horribly disfigured. Eventually there was a lawsuit and they tried to sue the guy who modified the airplane, as though he had something to do with it, but the suit was finally dropped. We avoided the suit because he hadn't touched our airstrip. It was such a horrible incident.

"To make things even harder to understand, he was an instructor; he was also a medical doctor. We had talked to him and told him not to land that way, but he tried and the minute he came in low with that amount of airspeed there was no possibility of escape. Once he settled in near the ground he was done. It just seemed inconceivable that they did not see me standing right in the centre of the runway waving them off.

"He had no possibility of escape; absolutely everything was against him. Besides his excessive speed, he was fighting ground effect, and had a tailwind pushing him. To make matters worse, the runway was downhill in that direction. I knew that he was going to crash; when you are a bush pilot you can size those things up instantly."

When I asked Dave if he would fly in those mountains again he responded thoughtfully.

"Oh, perhaps as a younger man I probably would. But my balance isn't as good as it used to be, and my eyesight isn't as good either. It's a young man's game. After flying for 20 years I figured I had pushed it long enough. But it isn't only that because the economic times had changed. The US dollar was dropping; fuel prices kept rising; wages were going up; but the revenues were dropping. I sold out to Leif Olsen in 2005. I flew for him for two more years. He also bought the ranch and everything else. All we took out was a bit of furniture."

Memories of guiding

At that point I asked Dave to talk about his guiding and how much he used horses.

"We had about 70 horses, which we kept at the ranch. We had six horses for each hunter and guide. So when we had 12 guides working, we needed 72 horses. I had a hair-raising experience myself when I was guiding. That was about 1983 or '84. I took out a mixed-bag hunter who had already got a sheep and a goat. So we moved across the highway to some good moose pasture. We were on horseback and it was a tough three-hour ride back in there. Well, we got a fine moose back in what we called Grizzly Gulch and while I was cutting it up, our horses started going crazy. We knew there was a grizzly in the thickets around us but we couldn't see it. We got the cape and the antlers off the moose and cut it up, and then I put a white piece of cloth on it so I could tell if there was a bear on it when we came back. By the time I got finished it was starting to get dark, so we had to get out of there. We got the horses loaded and headed out of that burn area, and I was sure happy to get out of there. When we got to a creek, I unloaded the cape and antlers and tied them up in a tree for pickup the next day.

"We carried on and it was so dark I could just make out the ears of my horse. When we got about one mile from our camp, my horse stopped and wouldn't go ahead. So I had just leaned forward to try to see what the problem was when my horse and I slid down into a creek, about an eight-foot drop. I got the wind knocked out of me and found the horse was lying on my right leg. It wasn't moving, so I thought it might be dead. My left leg was in front of the saddle horn and the horn was poking right into it, giving me a terrible cramp. Here I was lying in this creek with big boulders and I had no idea what happened. I knew my hunter was right behind me and I didn't want him to land on top of us so I shouted to him to stop and bring his horse over carefully. He came to me and managed to get my left leg free, but my right leg was throbbing terribly under about a 1,300-pound horse. The hunter tried to lift the horse's head to free me, but no dice. Then he tried to dig the rocks out but they were frozen.

"Just as the hunter was trying to drag my horse off me with his horse, my horse came to and tried to get up. A few times he came back on my leg which was hurting like blazes, but finally he made it up with the hunter's help. I got up and was surprised that I was still able to walk.

"The bank had given away and that had caused us to fall. The horse had hit its head against a big rock and been knocked cold.

Dave showing where he and the horse fell. Photo courtesy Dave Wiens.

It also had a rock pushed into its shoulder so it was lame. Well we got back to camp at midnight, ate supper, and then went to bed. The next morning I was so stiff I could not get out of bed for some time. Eventually we went back to the creek where I found my watch crystal. It had been forced out of my watch without getting broken. Also, it was obvious that my head had missed a boulder by only inches when we fell. When we went back to the moose carcass, the flag was down, so I knew a grizzly was on it. We could not see 20 feet in that jungle, so the bear got the moose. We picked up the antlers and cape from the tree and went home.

"I learned a valuable lesson that day. I asked my hunter if he would have known how to get help if I had died or not been able to get out from under the horse. He was certain he could not have found the way. From then on I made certain that my hunters knew they should point their horses in the right direction, then give them free rein, because they would go straight home."

I asked Dave to talk about experiences with grizzlies, especially in regards to his guides and the hunters.

Dave and the pack train. Photo Dave Wiens.

"Yes, one of my guides—Jim Fulton—was guiding a bear hunter when the hunter got three shots into a grizzly. They knew he was hit hard, but he got into the brush on them. As it was early in the day, they gave it some time to die. They ate lunch and then went back to find the bear. The guide was in the creek bottom with his wife following him, and the hunter was on the bank in fairly open country. They were moving along slowly, following the blood trail, when this bear attacked them from about 40 yards. The bear was coming so fast that the guide only got one shot away into a black ball, and then the bear was on him. The bear grabbed him by the hand that was on the trigger, and pushed the safety on. With his other hand, the guide grabbed it by the ear. When the bear changed its grip to his arm, the guide got the safety back off and dropped it.

"But now the guide had several puncture holes in his arm, hand, as well as some on his rear end. He was suffering from a number of wounds, as well as the shock of it all. The hunter had been so terrified he was no help at all. Jim's wife was behind him but couldn't do much. Well, they managed to get Jim to the cabin, which was nearby, and then his wife took a radio and climbed the mountain to try and get through to us. She radioed us about seven in the evening and we were all at the ranch. We just had hunters arrive and one had a sheep so we were getting started on a party. I had finished a beer when the call came in saying, 'Jim just got chewed up by a grizzly. We need help; can you come?'

"That was about all we could understand of the message, so I had no idea what the situation was. He could have had his guts hanging out for all I knew. I ran to the plane and counted out only five gallons of fuel, which I put in, because I wanted to fly in light. Once in the air, I gathered my thoughts and called Ellie at the ranch. I told her to get an ambulance to meet me at the highway when I came back out. I added that if it was really serious I would fly him right to the hospital in Fort Nelson.

"When I got to the camp, there were horses all over the runway, and this was a nasty little airstrip. I looked it over and thought I had 300 feet of clear runway and I hoped I could put it in there.

Jim's wife was still up on the mountain with the radio because it was a long ride back down. The hunter was in camp but he didn't think about the horses being on the runway. Anyway, I managed to put it down between the horses and the bushes. I taxied over to the camp and rushed in, not knowing what to expect. There was Jim, and he was still alive. I asked if it was life-threatening and he said he was good to go. I loaded him in the plane and flew him to the ambulance. We got him to the hospital before infection could set in, and Jim made it plain that the worst part of the whole ordeal was when they put the pressure washer in to flush out all those holes where the bear had bit him. He also had to have some work done on his thumb which was almost torn off.

"So you can see we had some learning experiences. We never lost anyone, but we had a few broken legs and things like that. For instance, one guy had just booked in on a 21-day hunt, and this was an elk, deer, moose, grizzly and black bear hunt. It was the first day of his hunt and he was running through the bush when his leg just snapped down by his ankle. He broke a tendon. He had to pay for the hunt but I brought him back so he got his money's worth.

"We spent a lot of money trying to get radio coverage to all our camps. Once satellite phones came out we bought them, and we spent huge dollars on them just for safety. On the other hand, I saved money by only having to fly into the camps when they had meat ready or needed supplies."

"I've got a moose story for you," Dave said. "One of my young guides was really getting into the swing of things when he and a hunter spotted a bull moose. They spotted it in the distance so he put his scope on it and asked the hunter if he was satisfied with the size. The hunter agreed and they started a long stalk. They worked for several hours to get into position at about 100 yards, and the guide was getting suspicious because the moose was still sleeping. He fixed the binoculars on it only to see a bird land on its antlers. They had stalked a dead moose. An examination showed that another moose had gored it right in the eyeball and the antler tip must have pierced its brain.

"We tried spring bear hunts but they were really difficult in our area. We couldn't find where the bears would hang up anywhere; they were always on the move.

"I remember a preacher we had from North Carolina just after I started guiding, so I had very little experience at that point. I wasn't even carrying a gun; I just had an axe. So we were out hunting all day, while my wife was in camp with our four- and six-year-old children, cooking and things. Well, when we got home we learned that a bear had been in camp all day digging in the garbage and it didn't pay any attention when Ellie banged pots and pans trying to drive it away. We should have stayed in camp and washed the laundry that day. As it turned out, the bear didn't try to bother her, although it came within 50 feet of the cabin.

"Anyway, we went out hunting again the next day and saw four bears. First we saw this bear a long way off; it was called the phan-

Resting the saddle horses. Photo Frank Cooke.

tom bear and was a huge grizzly. We went to the end of this valley and I looked up to see two bears—a boar and a sow. So we tied up our horses and got ready to head up after the big bear. Remember that I just had an axe and we were going up to two big bears. Just as we were leaving the horses, I looked back and there was another bear coming on the run. It was coming right to us from over in Peck's guiding area. It was not a huge grizzly, but I suggested to the hunter that we should take it. When the bear got right up to us, he fired; then we watched it take off. I told him to shoot again, and he kept shooting. It was right beside us and he couldn't hit it. The bear got away, and of course the big bears heard the racket, so they were gone and we got skunked.

"When we got back to camp, we put up a target and he couldn't hit it at close range. I looked at his gun and realized his scope was bent. We figured that the airline must have driven over it with the forklift; that was the only thing we could attribute it to. Imagine that, his scope was bent down so much that you could barely open the action, yet he hadn't even realized it."

I suggested that an anti-hunting airline employee did it, but that failed to explain how he could aim at that bear and not notice it.

"It seems impossible. Anyway, we straightened it out with an axe and got it to shoot on target. We had no other option than to get it working because no one was coming to check on us for 10 days. The end result was that we had a chance at four bears and ended up with none.

"We had a lot of bears in our area but in spring they were really hard to hunt. We didn't have good slides to hunt on and the high country was too rocky and hard to get around on."

When I asked Dave what would have happened if they shot a bear and then found it was eating on a carcass, his reply was straight to the point.

"They wouldn't believe you!"

I had to interrupt him to relate a case where many years ago, a guide shot a moose on the edge of a stream when he had two

American bear hunters with him. They tied it with wire so the bear couldn't drag it away and when the hunt was over, the hunters went to the Wildlife Branch and turned him in. They got away without paying, and the guide was forced to sell his area; so much for being mister nice guy. But he knew and broke the rules so it was time for new ownership.

"Once I guided a guy from New York," Dave began, "and we went out after moose. So we trucked on down this road to where I knew there was some good moose pasture. As we rode along, I heard this clicking sound behind me. I looked around and here he was riding along with his gun pointed right at my back and he was feeding cartridges into it. First off, he was lucky the horse didn't buck him off, and second, every time he closed the bolt it was cocked and ready to fire. If something touched the trigger, he would have blown me right off my horse. So I jumped off my horse, grabbed his rifle and took all his bullets and told him he would get them back when he needed them. I just couldn't believe it; that he could be such a rookie, so I decided to keep right close to him.

"We always wanted them to fire their guns to be sure they were lined up, but sometimes we missed. I had a guy come there and we took him to the gun range we had on the ranch. He fired from the table and the scope fell off his gun. He explained that he had just bought the rifle and they were supposed to put the scope on and line it up. So you have to check everything. We always had someone watching and it was easy to tell this guy was going to miss and this other person was good.

"Our guides had to protect themselves so they carried guns when they were specifically going after a bear. Most of the time our hunters were after sheep, elk or moose."

I asked what the guides would do if they were going back to a carcass to get meat or antlers or whatever. I wondered if they would trust their lives to the hunters.

At that point Dave started laughing and replied, "As long as we could run faster than they could. Also, if we left a carcass that we had to go back to, we always put a flag on top of it so that we could tell before we got close if a bear had touched it.

"On one trip I took this German hunter out and we got a moose right away, but he also wanted bear and caribou. This hunter was very impatient; he would glass for two minutes and then read a book. So we went out this one day and as soon as he started reading, I said, 'Did you see that moose?' He would look and start reading again, so I would say, 'Did you see that one?' I did that several times and then I spotted this massive grizzly.

"It looked like two bears. But it was its rump and then its huge belly that was almost dragging on the ground. So we made a stalk on it and got within 150 yards. We could hear the rocks rolling from its digging but we couldn't see it. It was in kind of a little gulch, so we waited and we waited and it was quiet. We couldn't walk in there because we could see maybe 20 feet at the most. Finally it started getting dark so we had to make a move. Our horses were tied about 150 feet behind us, so we walked back toward the horses. By that time I figured the bear had probably heard the horses and ran off. But just before we got to the horses we came upon fresh grizzly tracks; it had crossed between us and our horses. I looked at the tracks and I knew this was a different grizzly. It was getting close to dark and difficult to see in the fading light, so we rode back to camp and went back to the same spot the next day.

"As soon as we got there I spotted another bear. We watched it for a while until it went to sleep under a tree. We made a circle, got above it and started working our way down. That was when we found out that the brush was a lot thicker than we thought. We were in an old burn so there was a lot of dead brush to go through. This hunter was so clumsy he was breaking brush and making a lot of noise. Once he stepped on a large piece of debris and it make a loud snap, so I felt the hunt was over and the bear was long gone. Suddenly the bear got up right in front of me; somehow it had slept through all that noise. Oh, and I was carrying a 30-30. Anyway, the bear stood there looking at me while my hunter was coming down the hill about 20 feet behind me. I didn't dare turn

Russ Young with a broomed or broken-tip ram. Photo Dave Wiens.

around because the bear could have been on me in a second. I kept pointing at the bear and the hunter ran up behind me saying, 'What? What?' He hadn't even seen it. The bear took off over the edge of the hill, so I ran forward to try to find it again, while the hunter came as fast as he could. I got to the edge of the hill and the bear was out of sight. I could see a long way in both directions below me and no bear. I told the hunter to point his gun one way and I did the same the other way, in case of a charge. It didn't make sense—how could the bear disappear in three or four seconds unless it fell in a hole? We went right to the bottom of the hill and there was nothing. One thing for certain, every day is different out there and you never stop learning."

I offered to take a guess at what happened, because I knew of three similar events. One grizzly bear was in an open area when it was shot at and seemed to sense that it was trapped, so it rolled into a ball and bounced down the mountain at great speed and then stopped when it reached cover. That bear escaped and was back in the same area two weeks later. My brother Clarence shot at a grizzly high in the mountains and it made it into a small clump of trees in an open area. The men surrounded the trees and that bear vanished. Unless we believe in magic, that bear rolled down the mountain and escaped. That

Six-point elk, and happy, satisfied hunters.

same thing happened another time that I was aware of. Bears are a ball of muscle and can roll like a ball. But I know that it sure is spooky when they are close by and you see and hear nothing. As I was curious, I asked Dave to elaborate on any accidents they had during his years in the woods, aside from the guide getting mauled.

"We had some broken legs, sprained ankles and things like that. One guy had a heart attack, but we got him out and he survived. We also had some wranglers bucked off and hurt; things like that. But we were lucky because we never had anyone seriously hurt.

"We had a lot to look after, such as moving 70 horses and taking care of all the cabins; it sure kept us busy.

"I've got another story for you—we had this hunter arrive from Pennsylvania who raised chickens for McDonald's. His buddies were in another camp while he was hunting out of this one. He always carried this backpack with him, so when he got into camp, he just threw his pack on the ground. Well, his horse just freaked right out at this thing jumping off his back. The horse took off and the rider got his foot stuck in the stirrups and was getting dragged along. This was a big, strong 1,500-pound horse and it was bucking and kicking as it tore across the field. The guide was already off his horse, so he grabbed his rifle and was just going to try to shoot the horse when the guy's foot slipped out. The guy was banged up a bit and I wanted to take him for a medical check-up, but he wouldn't go. He said, 'I'm fine.'

"Just imagine if the guide had missed his shot and hit the hunter; or if the horse would have dropped on top of the hunter. We were more than lucky that time. He was just stiff and sore but he was okay.

"We also had a lady from Salt Lake City, Utah, who came on a hunt. She and her guide came to a steep hill where it was muddy and slippery. As they were hanging on to their saddles to help them up, her horse went right over backwards. When she landed the saddle horn was right in her belly. Her horse landed right on top of her and then rolled off. She had to be the luckiest person in the world, because her feet didn't get stuck in the stirrups. As it turned out, they had landed in a soft spot so the saddle horn did not penetrate her abdomen. It was a real mossy, soggy piece of ground where they landed and she was just buried in there. We dug her out and she was fine; she had no broken bones or serious injuries. It shows you that when you are working with horses anything can happen; it was a miracle because she could easily have been killed.

"Another time we had a client come on a grizzly hunt, as well as moose and elk. So they went fly-camping to this place we call Cairn Mountain. On the way in there they were riding up this long, steep hill, at least half a mile long, so it's a long pull. Suddenly a grizzly bear came out on the trail ahead of them and let out a roar. Well, everyone, including the guide, spooked so bad that they turned their horses around and took off down the mountain; that is, everyone except the hunter. His horse wouldn't move; she was our smallest horse, named Marsha, and she just froze up. That bear charged right at them and Marsha stood her ground. The hunter was beating on her but she wouldn't move. Well, when the bear got close, it veered and took off; probably puzzled by the action of the horse. After the bear left, the hunter said, 'We're going home; I've had enough!'"

I pointed out to Dave that I wanted the readers to take note of why the bear left when the horse didn't run. This shows that they can be bluffed by something that appears larger than them as long as it doesn't run. That's why I stress the importance of people taking off their jackets and holding them as high and wide as possible.

Dave agreed and told another story. "Once we had a guy from Europe and they were hunting moose and grizzly when they came upon this grizzly on a moose carcass. Maybe it was a carcass from a moose other hunters had taken or maybe the bear took it down; anyway, it was a massive bear. They started making a stalk on it when it disappeared from view. They carried on and when they spotted it again it was only 40 feet in front of them. The guide shouted for the hunter to shoot, because the grizzly was coming to them. The guy was working his gun but nothing was happening. Then the guide fired a shot and the bear took off into thick cover. We looked for that bear for a long time but we couldn't find it. We finally found it the next spring. It had been gut-shot and it went to the creek. We found its skull the next spring and it measured over two feet—a big bear. Well that guy was done bear hunting too!"

At that point I had to intervene. I suggested that since there is no possible way that anyone can know how a hunter is going to react when faced with a critical situation, changes need to be made. More emphasis should be placed on the guides because they are a known quantity. They should pack rifles at all times and have to pass accuracy tests. Then they should only give the hunter one shot before they react. The guide usually knows if the animal has been hit, and if it does not go down, he should put it down. If the hunter misses and the animal escapes, then let it go. I believe that the wounding of wildlife could be almost entirely eliminated by this one simple change.

Having been on the receiving end of grizzly charges, I know

they can come at breakneck speed and the guide should be in complete control of the situation. It is not good enough to have someone pumping live cartridges on the ground or repeatedly squeezing the trigger when there isn't a cartridge in the firing chamber. Probably most important of all, is that all bullets should have to meet certain standards. They should all have to open up completely in 12 inches of simulated flesh. Too much wildlife is lost because of bullets that travel clean through large animals without opening up. Accidents will always happen; bullets can ricochet and gut-shots may happen, but with the proper bullets the animal should die in 15 to 20 minutes or less.

The cost of guiding

Dave had a few more stories to share. "We had enormous insurance costs with the lodge, airplane, guides and all," he said. "Our insurance costs ran to about $25,000 a year. When we first bought the area, I had this dream that we would build a lodge on a little hill near our double-wide trailer. That dream came true in 1995 when we poured $800,000 into it. It had everything a hunter could think of and was our best asset when it came time to sell. As well, every window had a view; it was just perfect. The front window had a view of the runway so you could see the planes coming in and out. You could also see herds of elk and the hunters loved it."

Working together

"The people who took over from us didn't have any previous experience either. They did the same thing as us and went in cold turkey. So far they seem to be right on track. I'm sure it helped that I stayed and flew for them for two years while they got things figured out. But going in green has its advantages because you have no preconceived ideas. You learn things that the industry doesn't know. So people would come to us and say, 'That's a good idea!' Because of that, we ended up changing some things in the industry. It presented a new way of looking at things.

"I know that when we came in, everyone was complaining about the game wardens and politicians and how tough they were. So we went into the industry trying to work with these guys. It ended up that we had a positive influence by working with these people and getting things done together.

"We met with the wardens and asked them how they wanted to get things done; if they wanted us to report everything that went wrong. They said, 'Of course!'

"So we told them they had to make that possible; they had to believe us when we told them something. When it was an accident, they had to treat it like one.

"I'll give you an example—one of our guides was out sheep hunting and there was a big 40-inch ram up on a hill; a real beauty. The hunter shot at it and it fell down out of sight. The guide told him to reload and be ready, which he did. Then the ram stood up again in the same exact spot. The guide told him to shoot again and the ram dropped. When they got to the spot, they had two rams down; they had shot both of them. So, what to do? The guide dressed them out and brought them down to the highway; then called me and asked what he should do. I told him to bring them in and we turned them over to the Game Department. The man said, 'I'm really glad you brought them in; I will not give you a fine.'

"I asked for one of the sheep and he said, 'Oh, I can't let you have them. They were taken illegally.'

"The hunter was actually crying and I was just livid inside. I explained that the first ram was taken legally; the second one wasn't.

"He walked into the back for a few minutes, either to think things over or get a second opinion. Then he came back and said, 'You're right! Will you be willing to pay a $200 fine for the second sheep?'

"The hunter jumped at that and said he would pay anything because he just wanted his sheep.

"Anyway, that's how we built trust over situations like that. And every year there were similar instances, but we always came forward with the errors. Another time a hunter shot at a caribou. The guide could tell it was hit, but it managed to run into a thick clump of brush. The guide went on one side of the bushes and the hunter on the other. Then this caribou came running out with a blood spot on its side, so the hunter shot again. But it was not the same caribou, and it was not quite legal. So then they had two animals. What had happened was that the second caribou had rolled in the blood of the first one because they were in the rut. It had a big red spot on its side, so they looked identical, except the second one only had four points.

"So we took it in and the officer started laughing and admitted that he would have done the same thing. He even asked the hunter if he wanted the meat from the second bull.

"We couldn't believe it. He gave us the meat and no fine. So it paid off to be honest with them; after all, they were just doing their jobs. Every year we had stuff happen but we came forward with it and we built trust.

"Once we had a guide who was tempted into letting a hunter shoot an illegal sheep. He offered the guide $5,000 to let him, so the guide relented. When I found out, I turned them in. The guide and hunter got stiff fines, lost the sheep, and I fired the guide to boot. The guides all knew that if they had an accident they could turn it over to me and we would work it all out. If they hid something and I found out, they knew they were done. More importantly, the Game Department knew we were on the up and up.

"After Jim left, a new batch of wardens came in and the head guy was a real John Wayne type. They were laying for us at every turn. They had men on the mountains watching everything we did. It was disgusting, but they never got a thing on us. Finally they asked, 'How can you have so many things going wrong with your outfit year after year?'

"Of course I told them that we came forward with everything so we could deal on an honest footing with them. Anyway, the end result was that they finally left us alone.

"I remember an event that took place back in the '80s when

Fort Nelson was a rough town. It had two bars—the Trapline Hotel and the Fort Hotel; they had entertainment and all. Well, the hunters had heard of it and they sometimes would come a day early just to visit there, because you never knew what might happen. So this one young hunter came a day early and went to the Trapline Hotel. We don't know what happened; maybe he got drunk and fell, or else he got into a fight, because he ended up with a broken leg. He had about $12,000 into this hunt and he wound up with a broken leg. He was too embarrassed to talk about it, so we never found out what happened that night. I can't help but wonder what he told his wife. He had to pay for the hunt because all the expenses were made and the space was taken up so we couldn't advertise for a last-minute hunt. I felt sorry for him, but he created the problem. Anyway, he did come back; I managed to get him in on a cancellation where he didn't have to pay the full price. He managed to get his sheep—in fact, he got a 43-inch ram, so that must have made up for the earlier failed hunt.

Showing off the trophies. Photo Dave Wiens.

"You know it is sad when a good guide gets too old to guide anymore. Dave Ronquist was such a guide; he grew up in Cremona, Alberta, and went to the Northwest Territories. In fact, he was one of the first guides in that area. He guided up there for over 20 years before he came and guided for us. Then he worked for us for about 15 years. By that time he was around 65 years old. When the season was over we were having a couple of beers and he told me, 'Dave, I can't see, I can't pee and I don't know where I'm at anymore. I think I have to quit.'

"He had tears in his eyes because he knew he was done. The last few years I always sent a wrangler with him to help out with things like cutting meat and helping with the horses. He was a great guide."

A close call

"I have a story about running into a bear with four cubs. Lots of times we saw three cubs, but after we started the wolf-control program we started seeing families with four cubs. I hated it, because that meant we had far too many bears. Anyway, I was guiding a big fellow named Dan from California, and he weighed about 275 pounds. Well, as you can imagine, it was hard work for the horse to carry this man. Anytime we had to climb a steep hill, he had to get off and grab the horse's tail to help pull him up.

"We were hunting sheep and he always played out so we couldn't get close to one. We gave it a good try and finally gave up. Then we went hunting moose in a place called Grizzly Gulch, and you can guess the reason for that name. We got into this meadow area and sure enough, we spotted some moose there including a big one that had six points up front on one side. So he shot at the moose and I could tell he was hit because I saw his head whip around, but he didn't go down. I told the hunter to shoot him in the hump, and that put him down. I proceeded to skin the moose but I was puzzled because I couldn't find any blood. Finally, as I caped around the head I found a bullet hole in his eye. Then I found another hole in the other eye; somehow the bullet went through both eyes without breaking an eyelid.

"I used to pack out the cape and the antlers with me, and I would chop out the brain cavity so that the antlers would fit right over the saddle horn, Then I would put a stick behind the saddle so the paddles of the antlers would fit there. Anyway, I had a hunter with me and I was riding my horse through this big burn area when we got down to a creek. At once I noticed fresh grizzly tracks made by a sow with cubs. I knew they had just come up out of the creek because the rocks were still dripping wet. This was a bad deal because they were ahead of us and we were heading into a narrow canyon, and when I say narrow, I mean the bottom of this canyon wasn't 100 feet wide. We had no other choice but to go on because that was the only way back to camp. I was riding on the horse with all the antler tips pointing up at me and I realized that if the horse bolted and the bear didn't get me, the antlers probably would. I got off to lead the horse and told the hunter to put a cartridge in the chamber and to be sure to leave the safety on. We had to hurry and get through before dark, so we were walking along and my horse started snorting. At the same time I noticed that the bears had turned off and started climbing the ridge. My eyes were looking everywhere and then I spotted her about 300 yards up the hillside and she had four little cubs with her. I told my hunter not to stop—we had to keep going. Suddenly the sow charged down the hill at us and there I was without a gun. It was an anxious moment, but she stopped about halfway to us and stood up. She watched us pass and then she went back up to her cubs. She wasn't very big but she sure meant business.

"Luckily for us, the horses didn't panic, they just kept on moving, but I'm telling you that my heart was doing a number that time. It was a good thing she was between us and her cubs, but had the situation been reversed, it could have been a bad scene."

I mentioned to Dave that I had learned the hard way that mother grizzlies are much more protective of their young during their first year. I asked him if he had ever watched two bull moose fighting.

"Yes, I was guiding a sheep hunter and we were just above timberline. I heard a moose grunting so I looked and there was a moose walking along the trail. And then I heard another moose coming from the other end of a meadow, where they met. And instantly they charged each other, locked antlers and started going round and round. One would push the other and then the other one would push back; they wanted to kill each other. All at once one of them broke free and took off with the other one in hot pursuit. The one in the lead was all humped up and trying to avoid getting antlers up his rump, while the back one was doing his best to get rid of the competition.

"I could see that entire area and there wasn't a cow there anywhere, so that shows how ready they are to do battle."

Animal epidemics

"One of our biggest problems for many years was porcupines. In the early days it became an epidemic. For instance, we couldn't leave our saddles hanging over a log overnight. If you left your boots outside overnight you would have nothing to wear by morning. We had guides who learned that lesson the hard way. We had saddles partly eaten and the horses' reins eaten up. Anything that contained salt was eaten up. We were building cabins at that time in the high alpine and one of them was built with plywood. We flew the supplies in by helicopter, which was really expensive, and we were up killing porcupines all that first night. They were trying to eat the plywood before we could even use it, so we had to kill six porcupines that night. Even the next day while we were building, they kept coming in and we had to keep killing them. So we had to put tin on the outside four feet up in order to protect the plywood.

"One fall a resident hunter left our ladder leaning against the cabin and a porcupine got up there and ate his way through the wall. Then he went to work and ate all the plywood from the inside out. So we still had the two-by-four structure, but all the plywood was gone.

"I recall the time I went hunting in a place we called Yash Creek, up in the alpine. Well, the porcupines love to run around at night, and we were camping in one of those tents with one side open. We were in our sleeping bags when I noticed a porky coming into our tent. I chased it down and got it with an axe. A while later I awoke to find a porky in the tent with us. My wrangler, Red Cloud, was sleeping and the porky was right by his face. I told Red Cloud not to move because there was a porky right by his face. I eased myself around behind it and slowly drove it out of the tent. I chased it down and went to hit it with the axe, and in the dim light I drove my hand right down on top of a tent peg. The porky climbed a tree so I threw the axe at it and missed. I heard a tinkling sound and the next day I found my axe where it landed on the gravel bar, so I ended up with a dull axe and a very sore hand.

"I had to kill two the first night, three the next and four the third night. That's the way it went in there in the early years. I have a piece of tin that the porcupines routed the edges of and it is beautiful. An artist painted a scene on it of the elk and sheep my two daughters got; it is a work of art. Anyway, the porcupines were thick like that for about 10 years and then they were gone. That's a good thing, because they were like a plague—if you left your bike or snowmobile unattended, when you returned the handle bars, seat and wiring would be gone.

"We had another plague one year. The rabbits were so thick that they were getting run over on the highway in droves. The road actually got slick from so many getting killed. That was about 1980. The next year they got diseased and most were wiped out.

"There is still an abundance of marmots in those mountains. When we would go sheep hunting up in the alpine they were a pain in the neck. They were always watching and they alerted the sheep. They would all start whistling and the sheep knew what that meant; the animals understand each other. A big ram would look down and hear all the fuss and away he would go. In some of those valleys there were so many marmots that there was no point in hunting there. The bears used to dig them up quite a lot."

I mentioned to Dave that I used to watch the bears dig for them, but some of the marmots got quite smart and dug in under large boulders. Sometimes the bears moved a mountain of earth for nothing.

I wanted to know what the greatest downside and upside of those years in the guiding business were for Dave.

"The downside was the constant pressure that was on my shoulders. I always worried that if I happened to get injured the results could be catastrophic. I had to do all the flying and the paperwork and the planning; sometimes it weighed me down. The greatest part of it was that you were daily living a life of constant adventure in a place where few people ever go. And there is freedom; I mean total freedom. It's a world of unparalleled beauty that some call God's Country."

MEMORIES OF THE WILD

My brother Clarence

There is one day I'll never forget and it concerns my first grizzly bear hunt with my brother Clarence. We had practised on a few black bear and then decided to try for a grizzly. One day we got word that a grizzly was feeding on a moose less than a mile from the community, so that was our big chance. We didn't have a clue how to go about it, so we ventured to the home of a retired trapper named Fred Rankin. We described the situation to him and asked his advice and I'll never forget his response: "Oh, just go for the kill and make lots of noise. He'll come out!"

Well, I can't speak for Clarence, but that was not at all what I had wanted to hear, although this demonstrated the total respect many of the old-time woodsmen had for grizzlies.

We figured that we had to start somewhere, so away we went, Clarence with a worn-out .32 special and yours truly with a 30-30. The moose was on a hillside just above a stream, so we had no trouble finding where the bear had been coming down to drink. We followed his trail up the hill and over the top a short distance where we came to a clearing about 15 feet across with a pile of earth and a few logs on top. Suddenly we spotted some moose legs sticking out of the pile and realized that we were in the grizzly bear's kitchen.

At that instant I felt some big-time shivers running up and down my spine. We looked this way and that, expecting a charge at any moment, but there was only silence. Perhaps luckily for us the bear had decided to go for a stroll, and that is why it buried the carcass. We never heard a sound, so I'm sure the bear was not nearby. Did we wait for the bear? Not the way I remember it; I think we figured we had done our part and we headed for home.

I suppose many people have had to meet the challenge of getting a cat down out of a tree. In my case it was a big tomcat that was right in the top of a spruce tree. Since I refused to go up into the tiny top of the tree, and since it simply refused to move, we had a stalemate. As luck would have it, Clarence was plowing snow off the roads with his D6 Cat and when he arrived I explained the situation to him. He quickly said that he knew how to get it down. He took his Cat and bumped the tree in an effort to dislodge it, but the Cat held on tight. Finally, Clarence took a bit of a run at the tree with his cat and it broke off. Down came our cat, riding the tree until it was near the ground, at which point it jumped and landed safely in the snow. Then with a few mighty bounds, it disappeared under one of my sheds. The moral of the story is that whenever our little cat heard the big Cat coming, even in the distance, it took refuge under that shed.

I think it is only fair I tell you about one that backfired on me. When I was a young lad, I owned part of a Dodge pickup. The reason I say "part of" is because there was a lot of parts missing and the ones that were left didn't work all that well. Since the starter was missing, that meant that I had to crank it by hand to start it, and that involved getting slapped a few times when it backfired. One day I found a starter that would fit my pickup; all I had to do was put it on and hook up the wiring.

Big John Humphreys and my brother Clarence were on hand for the big moment, so when I was ready to try it out, I shouted, "Here goes nothing!"

Harbouring a deep sense of pride at my mechanical accomplishment, I pushed the starter button expecting the starter to engage, but instead the horn honked. Was I embarrassed? Oh yes, and my two companions didn't let me forget that debacle for a good many years.

~

I suggest you put the children to bed before you read this story.

Clarence was always up to some kind of devilry. If anyone doesn't agree with that statement, just ask his wife, Olga. There was the day Clarence was out disking a field and plotting at the same time. When he came into the house for lunch he stated, "I think I'm going to quit this darn disking."

Quick as a wink Olga asked, "Why?"

Without even a trace of a smile, Clarence said, "Because it is killing all the orgasms in the soil!"

Being a schoolteacher, Olga bit and returned, "Orgasms, you mean organisms!"

Clarence's obvious reply: "No, I mean orgasms; you know, all those f------ worms."

~

Clarence really liked to pull jokes on people. Just the other day we were reminiscing and recalled one in particular that occurred about 55 years ago. It was a Sunday evening at our parents' home and we had just finished eating our evening meal, and as usual on a Sunday, Mom had just fed a mob of people.

One family in attendance had brought their little baby along, so this spurred Clarence to action. After dining, he retreated to the living room and seated himself on the chesterfield. Only a dim light entered the room from the light in the kitchen, so this offered a golden opportunity. Lying beside him, Clarence noticed a doll, so he placed a blanket over it, and then called big John Humphreys into the room. Before John's eyes could adjust to the dim light, Clarence asked him to sit down because he wanted to have a talk with him. John agreed, and was in the process of sitting right on top of the doll when Clarence shouted, "Oh my God, the baby!"

Clarence and Olga Boudreau. Note Clarence's evil grin.

Unable to stop his downward motion, John sat on the doll and then with a tremendous leap, landed right in the centre of the living room floor. I don't want to remember the words that emanated from John's mouth when he realized he had been had, but I am certain the doll blushed.

Clarence recalls the time that Dad came to inform him that the electric fence that surrounded the ranch was not working. (At the time Dad was not aware that his rubber boots prevented him from feeling the current.) Clarence responded by saying he had checked it just a short time earlier and it had been working then. Dad insisted, so together they went to check the fence during a rainstorm. When they arrived, Clarence touched the fence wire with one hand and lightly touched the tips of some grass with the other hand. He then informed Dad that he could feel the current passing through.

Still not convinced, Dad grabbed the wire with one hand and had just grabbed a handful of wet grass with his other hand when the wet felt hat on his bald head touched the top wire. In other words, Dad got the load from the wires and grounded it in the wet grass through his bald head. Clarence told us that when Dad came back down to earth, he acknowledged that there was indeed a goodly supply of juice in the wires.

To give a better idea of just what kind of a sense of humour Clarence possesses, I must include the tale of the watch. When we were just children my father had an old railroad quality pocket watch that he gave up on because it had died and gone on to keep time in heaven. So as a pastime we kids would take it apart and play with it while attempting to get it going again. Throughout the years more and more parts went missing. Not essential parts, just things like gears, the main spring and the hands. As well, the case got pounded in here and there during our repair work. Well, the years flew by until one evening in the 1960s, Clarence was perusing *The Family Herald* when he ran into one of those once-in-a-lifetime million-dollar deals—an ad that read, "Omar's Watch Clinic—I will repair any watch for $5.00."

This was a horrible blunder on Omar's part, and it became instantly apparent that he had not dealt with the Boudreau clan before.

Clarence knew another person who owned a Studebaker watch that could have arrived on the *Mayflower*; this watch didn't run either. So he bundled up the two watches along with another dead watch and all the pieces he could find and shipped them off with $15.00 to Omar in Winnipeg.

Poor Omar. Although he didn't realize it, he was about to experience a few bad-hair days.

Some time passed and then the watches arrived, along with a note that read, "Someone has been tempering with watch. Watch is a hell of a mass. Do not temper with watch."

Well, Omar kept his word about fixing the watches, because one watch ran for a week before it died and the others were stillborn. He fixed them alright. If memory serves me right, that $5.00 guarantee disappeared from the paper soon after. I mean, how could Omar have been sure there wasn't another Boudreau clan around somewhere?

Back in the late 1960s, I was postmaster in the tiny town of Penny, BC. At the same time I had a contract to meet mail trains in the dead of night. One evening an elderly gentleman bailed off the passenger train with only a few possessions. He asked if there was some accommodation available and I assured him that there was none. He asked if I could assist him the following day to find something and I promised to try. With that, he spent the night in the railway station.

The next day I moved him and his few possessions into a cabin that was available. I rounded up a few items necessary for his survival and left. A few days later he caught the train to Prince George where he bought a few groceries and a substantial amount of booze. The same evening I met the train and hauled him back to the cabin.

The following day I went to check on him and found him lying shivering on the cabin floor. Beside him lay the remains of what had been a 26-ounce bottle of whiskey. I made a fire and got the place warmed up, and then helped get him to the sofa, which was his only bed, and departed.

A few days later I went to his cabin and found him in a state of shock. I asked him what was wrong and he replied, "There was gunfire around here this morning!"

I tried to comfort him by saying, "That was my brother Clarence shooting at a coyote that was after his chickens!"

He let out a long sigh of relief and came back with, "Oooh, that's what it was; I thought maybe they were shooting at drifters or one thing and another!"

Just what that man had experienced and where he came from I never knew, but I sure wondered how he managed to reach the apparent age of late seventies. A short time later he left town and moved on to other adventures.

Animal tales

Throughout the years that I have spent gathering information for books, I have heard many almost unbelievable stories. Some appeared to be serious at the time, but turned out to be humorous in the end.

This story was told to me by an elderly trapper named Orv Prather. Late one evening at his cabin he walked outside to 'water the roses,' as he put it. Just as he got the fountain flowing, a bear jumped up right beside him. It had been lying against the side of the cabin only a few feet away and just out of his view. As my dad and I listened intently, expecting a confrontation, Orv laughed and explained that both he and the bear were equally startled and went their separate ways at about the same rate of speed. I couldn't resist asking if he had put it away before it stopped spraying, but he ignored me. Instead he thought about it for a moment and then added, "I think it came to listen to the 10 o'clock news."

Once again I asked if he had time to shut the fountain off before he put it away, but he just changed the subject. I took that as a no.

The porcupine affair

The following story was told to me by a guide of the fair sex on the condition that I not reveal her name. I don't like doing things this way, but perhaps the reason for anonymity will be clear. Why? It seems that along with another guide they were in a hurry to get their cabin erected so they had improvised by building an open-air outhouse. They didn't want to take time from their cabin building to erect a proper toilet, which they planned to build later.

One day as they were busy working on their cabin she felt the urge and made a run for the makeshift toilet. She no sooner flopped down on the improvised toilet seat when she received a sharp stinging sensation on her bum. She had sat down inches above a porcupine that was dining on their droppings. Seventeen was the number of quills extracted with great difficulty from her bottom, and lucky she was to have had a partner with her to remove the ones that were out of her line of vision. Did he rub salt in her wounds, so to speak? You bet, and although she did manage to see the humour in it, she blushed something awful and made it doubly plain that people had better not find out it was her that "got the point," as her partner put it.

I tried to make her feel better by explaining that I came within a whisper of having the exact same thing happen, and I only avoided disaster because I heard the animal moving. We had left too large a hole in the back of the outhouse, which we had deliberately left open to the Columbian ground squirrels that absolutely love eating those goodies along with the toilet paper. I pointed out that it could happen to anyone who does not check before they sit down in a makeshift open-air toilet. Point well taken?

One day I was climbing up toward timberline when I heard a gnawing sound up ahead. My first thought was beaver, but there was no water for at least a half a mile. I snuck ahead slowly and came upon a porcupine chewing an old moose antler. Apparently they love to dine on shed antlers as it must add a bit of calcium to go with the plywood, vinyl seats, engine hoses, wiring, billy cans, leather mitts, boots, saddles, toilet droppings and other debris they gorge on.

When we were lads, we heard porcupines were protected. Apparently that was just a gentleman's agreement, because no law concerning this has been found. The reasoning behind it was because they were animals a lost person was able to kill with a rock or a stick in order to prevent starvation. Wouldn't it have made more sense if Franklin's grouse, spruce grouse or fool hens, as they are commonly known, were protected? I recall that as boys we were able to walk right up to them and we got lots of them with our slingshots. In one instance, my brother Joe got two with a pitch fork. They were almost as smart as lynx or caribou.

Another special memory of mine was when my brother Clarence got his first grizzly bear. This was the oddest bear in that it had the most pronounced dish face I have ever seen anywhere. I challenge anyone to show me a more pronounced one.

Clarence with dish-faced grizzly bear.
Photo Clarence Boudreau.

Chasing the bears

Here's a story that was told to us children many times by my father. The year was about 1940, and the place was a logging camp owned and operated by Sinclair Mills. In those days, all the leftovers from the kitchen were thrown on a nearby dump. This attracted a great number of black bears, which in turn created an entertaining sport called, "Chasing the Bears." As there were fewer grizzlies around at that time, the men didn't worry about them, and they had not been seen at the dump. Anyway, one evening just after they finished their meals, one of the men shouted, "The bears are back, let's go chase them!"

Unknown to the men, the cook had gone to the dump that very afternoon and put up a cable noose, to catch a bear for some unknown reason. Well, my dad said that when they left the cookhouse, Oliver Prather was the man in the lead, but a few seconds later when they returned, Oliver was also in the lead, running flat out. What happened? One of the biggest bears ran into the noose; it swung out to its limit, and then came right back at the men, who thought they were being attacked. And what was the result? That was the end of the new-found sport, known for a short time as "Chasing the Bears."

Dog lovers should enjoy these stories told to me by Stan Bell, a retired railroad engineer. He and his partner, Dawn, were parked in a campsite at Goose Lake, north of Prince George, when they had a rather odd experience. In an adjacent campsite was another couple with a large dog they had named Ben. This couple had somehow trained Ben to pack pieces of firewood from the surrounding woods to their campsites in order not to have to buy firewood.

Everything went well until Stan caught Ben stealing his firewood. But Stan had an ace in the hole, so to speak, because he had brought a box full of wood from home, to be certain he had dry wood to start his campfire. What Stan didn't know was that Ben had been hiding in the woods watching him take the wood out of the box.

Note the cherry blossom ball that the bear didn't care for. Photo Stan Bell.

Well, the capper came when Stan caught Ben in the act of lifting the top off his wood-box and packing the wood back to his own campsite. The other couple understood what had happened and soon came to his campsite carrying the wood Ben had stolen. Then both couples sat back and had a hearty laugh about the situation, while Stan and Dawn both marvelled at the intelligence of the dog.

Stan and Dawn had another story that concerned a black bear; an event that also took place at Goose Lake. Apparently the bear was attracted to the Forest Service campsite because some well-meaning attendant had placed a cherry blossom deodorant ball inside the outhouse. Well, as the picture shows, the bear tore the wall off the outhouse and found the ball. But Bruno didn't like the taste of it, because the bear no sooner bit into it, when he turned and high-tailed it back out of the campsite. Perhaps someone should check further—maybe these balls will keep bears out of our communities.

Mysterious discoveries

When people spend a lot of time in the woods they are bound to stumble onto strange finds. Without a doubt one of the strangest I ever heard of came from my friend Herb Metzmeier of Terrace, BC. Herb was fishing Red Mountain Creek at Penny, BC, when he ventured above what is called The Falls. This is a tight canyon with near-vertical slopes. Imagine his surprise when he came upon a moose and grizzly bear. Both were dead, and they were lying side by side in about three feet of water. The moose was a young bull, and the bear was full grown with a beautiful coat. It was impossible to skin the bear in its position, so Herb had no choice but to walk away. He told me that he puzzled on what could have happened to them and finally decided that the bear had attacked the moose up above a cliff, and in an effort to escape, the moose had plunged both over the cliff to their deaths.

Herb Metzmeier.

An odd situation developed about 35 years ago in my hometown of Penny, BC. A local pioneer named Victor Mellows was falling some cedar trees in midwinter when he stumbled into a surprise. Inside a hollow cedar tree he found a ball of dormant mosquitoes. From what he told me, the ball was about 10 inches in diameter, so we can only marvel at the number of insects involved. Hundreds of thousands would be my guess, and that could be a conservative figure. Perhaps this is not uncommon, but it is the only time I have heard of such a thing.

I recall back in my school days when I collected several hundred mosquitoes and kept them in my dry inkwell. They hardly even covered the bottom, so imagine the number contained in the ball Victor found.

When I was a lad wandering the mountains I often heard hooting sounds and couldn't figure out what was making them, although I thought they were made by an owl. Sometimes I went in search of the origins of the sounds but when I got close, they fell silent. Then one evening I was sitting by a campfire with retired guide-outfitter Arne Jensen, as we were in the process of building heliports in the mountains at the time. I asked him what was making that noise and he replied, "I don't know; I've heard it many times but never found out what it was."

Once again I went in search of it and finally lucked out when I heard a hoot right on the other side of the tree I was standing beside. I stepped around the tree and there was a blue grouse sitting on a limb. I walked back to our campsite and told Arne what I found and he had a good laugh about it. I admitted that they had fooled me for several years as well until I caught this one in the act.

Another weird sound, somewhat like people clapping their hands together come from a herd of caribou running through snow. When their hooves go down into the snow, they spread apart to give the animals' feet a snowshoe effect. Then when they lift their hooves, the sides of their hooves come together to make the clapping sound. If there are many caribou involved, it can make a surprising amount of noise.

One evening while I was sitting in a cabin in the subalpine, I heard two men talking in low voices as they approached the cabin. I opened the door to see who was there and they turned into two porcupines. The sounds were identical. Similarly, I heard two men muttering in low voices as they followed the stream I was sitting beside. It was hunting season, so I assumed it was two hunters. Imagine my surprise when they entered a small clearing and turned into a black bear with two cubs. I guess she was teaching them the ways of the wild.

Fish tales

Fisher-folks should be able to relate to this next story. It started when my brother Joe invited me out to his cabin at Cluculz Lake west of Prince George. The purpose for the trip was to try for some big char, which the lake is famous for. We set off in his boat and let out a great amount of line, because we knew these lunkers would be down deep at that time of year. After fishing for about an hour, I was rewarded with a tremendous strike and knew I had the grand-daddy on my line. I slowly fought it up toward the surface while my brother was oohing and aahing. What puzzled me was why this creature kept going back and forth in a sawing motion. Joe kept cheering me on and I finally worked it up to where it was right under the boat. When it broke the surface, we quickly brought it into the boat and couldn't believe what we had caught—a grey fish just over three feet in length. I had hooked a piece of limb right in the centre, and that was why it kept going in one direction and then the other. The moral of the story was that Joe nailed that fish to the wall of his cabin with the hook and a piece of line dangling from it. We both believe it was the all-time record fish to come out of that lake, and what a heroic fight it put up.

Here's another fish story to chew on. Back in the 1950s I walked into Slim Lake with my friend Herb Metzmeier; our mission was to cut trail in the area for the Forest Service. In the evenings we would do a bit of fishing, planning to take them home when the job was finished. We kept them alive in a wooden crate that was placed underwater. One evening we managed to land two large bull trout but this presented us with a problem—how to prevent the fish from spoiling. A tiny spring ran into the lake right beside us, so we followed it into the woods a short distance where we dug a pool in the soft black earth and then put the trout in. We left after issuing them a stern warning, "Don't go away!"

When our trail cutting was finished and we were on our way home, we stopped to pick up the fish only to find the pool empty. Just as we were leaving, Herb spotted a tail fin sticking out of the black earth. We started digging and found both fish alive and well. They must have realized how vulnerable they were and took protective measures by digging down out of sight in the soft, black earth. Who says fish are stupid? I mean, they don't go to school for nothing.

Stan Hale

The following story concerns pack train operator Stan Hale when he reached the young age of 80 years. At the time, he was living in a house trailer at a horse ranch just south of Quesnel, BC. I had taken along a few pictures of old-time trappers and woodsmen that I wanted him to try to identify, and although he could not help much with that because of waning vision, he did help me with a few more stories. At one point in our conversation, I asked him if I could see some of the pack train photos from his years in the woods. Stan told me that he did not even have a picture of himself; they had all been lost in a fire.

A few weeks later I returned to visit Stan, seeking some more information. As we chatted, I pulled out an enlarged, framed photo and handed it to him, asking if he knew the two people displayed therein. Stan took the photo, glanced at it and then I spotted a few tears running down his cheeks. It was a picture of himself and trail-hand Carl Anderson at Slim Lake during early summer 1951. They were heading to Barkerville with a pack train of horses to meet the Army Topographical Engineers. I told Stan that the photo was a gift and the next time I went to visit him, the picture was proudly displayed on the living room wall. Somehow, despite numerous moves, that one picture I had taken at Slim Lake over 50 years earlier, had managed to survive the rigors of time.

My favourite story from Stan was the time on these surveys when they got a visitor in their camp while they were absent. It was a grizzly bear that ate the toes out of a pair of boots, then ate half a box of dynamite and left.

Back in the '40s a man named Bud Fuglem resided in the area of Crescent Spur, just west of McBride, BC. Perhaps 50 years later he related a story to me about the wedding of Stan Hale at a private home in the tiny community of Snowshoe. It was about three o'clock in the afternoon as the wedding was winding down when Stan was asked, "Do you take this woman to be your lawfully wedded wife?"

Stan replied, "I do!"

At that exact instant the clock on the wall chimed out, "Cuckoo! Cuckoo! Cuckoo!"

Instantly the entire room full of people broke into uncontrollable laughter. This was a story that would be told and retold along the railway line east of Prince George for many years thereafter.

Loading ties at Hulatt. Photo Eric Davidson.

When reminiscing about days gone by, the subject comes up about the strength of people in our fathers' time. Often the stories seem hard to believe in our present-day roles as couch potatoes. One story with supporting proof can be seen in the accompanying photo. It shows men, Carl Davidson of Prince George among them, loading switch ties into boxcars. This took place at Hulatt, a railroad stop east of Vanderhoof during 1925. These were green timbers, and being that I was a licensed scaler, I realize that each tie weighs about 300 pounds. Is it any surprise that many of these tie hackers, as they were called, suffered from severe shoulder problems? Another thing, show me three good men who can lift, load and pack these massive ties up a ramp, and I will buy you a coffee.

Fire on the mountain

For over forty years I was a firefighter and was attendant on hundreds of wildfires, and as a consequence, I spent a great deal of time in helicopters. Many times I was let off in the alpine and had to fight my way down the mountainside to fires. It was a challenging and sometimes dangerous job, but the adventure made it all worthwhile.

I recall the time I went to fall a large burning cedar tree with Allan Spoklie. When the tree started to fall it broke halfway up

Jack dropping a burning cedar tree at a wildfire. Photo Allan Spoklie.

where it had nearly burnt off. Then the bottom portion of the tree gave the top portion an extra kick. This resulted in the bottom portion of the top piece landing 100 feet from the trunk. At a time like that, one doesn't know which way to move to get to safety. Many fallers have been killed in similar circumstances.

Often it was impossible to fall a burning cedar tree because they are all hollow inside. As soon as the saw cut was started, fire rushed out the cut and forced the faller away. Searching for a way to deal with this situation, I invented a nozzle that does just that. As well, it handles fires inside walls. Because of this I won a monetary reward from the Ministry of Forests.

The nozzle works in this fashion: the faller inserts the chainsaw on a 45-degree upward angle to the inner core of the tree; then the narrow nozzle slides into the saw cut and water is used to cool down the entire lower part of the tree. This allows the faller to proceed. The nozzle accommodates foam as well, so this is a quick, safe solution to what had been an endless problem.

Firefighting has changed so much since I was a lad. Many times we arrived at a fire that was burning so intensely that we just sat around and rested until around midnight. Then, as the fire died down in the wee hours, we attacked with a vengeance. Everything was in our favour that way, and we often had the fire out or under control before the sun came up.

Since that time, ground crews have been rendered impotent and often sit all day waiting for a ride back to camp. The air division has taken control in BC. Fortunes worth of tax dollars are wasted because the new regulations do not allow firefighters to enter the fire area until all the danger trees are down. Since the fallers cannot walk on fire, they cannot drop the danger trees; hence there is a stalemate and the crews sit around all day. We always went into the fire area as a group, and if it was a large fire, we cooled things down with water so the fallers could do their work.

Firefighting costs could be drastically reduced by hiring the initial attack employees by the month. At present there is little desire to put the fires out. The gold is in all the overtime that can pile up. And above all else, expert power-saw operators are all-important. Present-day attack crews often hire beginners for these jobs.

It is so nice to see progress, especially if it puts fortunes into the hands of a few. The show looks good with the air tankers and helicopters slinging bucket loads of water, but with the exception of low brush fires, few fires have ever been put out that way.

I recall taking an initial attack crew with me to a fire. I was informed via radio that this fire had already been hit by the air tankers. When we got to the fire, I could not find any evidence of the retardant, so I called district office and informed them of the fact, at the same time suggesting that the air tankers had missed their target. They let me know that this fire had indeed been hit by the tankers. I searched around and eventually found a few drops of retardant on some leaves and bushes. At least 99 percent of the retardant had hung up in the heavy canopy and had failed to reach the ground where all the heat and fire was. In other words, they can drop all the retardant they want, but eventually some ground troops have to go in and put the fire out. Otherwise they could end up with a summer-long project, a lot of lost forest, and tremendous expense to the tax-payers.

Ace pilot Dan Wiebe took us into some tight places with his helicopter. Photo Allan Spoklie.

My best memories with the Forest Service involved chopper pilot Dan Wiebe; the tight places he landed me in saved countless miles of walking. Often he dropped me off within 50 yards of a fire, telling me he could put me closer but the rotor wash would fan the fire. The Hughes 500C, or 500D are the best initial attack helicopters ever invented. Just imagine travelling 140 miles an hour and then being dropped off right beside a fire, or let off on any alder thicket.

I frequently had to climb up mountains, or descend down through cliffs and brush, carrying at least 65 pounds with my chainsaw and other equipment, but with the Hughes I never once had to walk even half a mile. This meant I would arrive at the fires with energy to fight the fires, rather than exhausted from fighting the mountains. The speed in getting to fires means there is far less chance of escapes.

The first years I fought fires we got the princely sum of 33¢ an hour, so there was no desire to hang around longer than necessary. As stated, we often sat around and rested during the day and waited until late evening when the fires would die right down. Then we would attack with a vengeance when everything was in our favour. We would keep some fires going inside the guards to provide adequate light for us to see and we usually had the fires contained or out by sunrise.

The 19 firefighters lost in the Arizona fires shows the importance of having the crews in safe places during the day when the fires are most apt to travel. Firefighting at night is not allowed anymore because it is too dangerous. I beg your pardon! It is far safer, with the exception of high winds creating falling snag situations. As stated, the winds and the fires often die down at night and this allows a safer and far more effective means of fighting right at the fire perimeters, and thereby stopping the all-important leading edges of the fires. I recall a fire we attended on a steep slope. It was too hot to get to the leading edge so we cut poles about 12 feet long, put a crosspiece in front of it and kept raking the leading edge of the fire back into itself. By sunrise we had the fire under control. Fighting fires during the daylight hours often means chasing the fires rather than attacking the leading edges. It is just too dangerous to place the firefighters ahead of, or above a large fire in high or extreme conditions during the day.

Often lessons are learned the hard way, such as building a helipad above or downwind of a fire. Just when you may need it for an emergency medivac, it may be going up in flames. Another tip is to always fall burning snags up or down the slope; a snag felled across the slope can break and send burning portions bouncing down the slope to start a fire far below—a dangerous situation in high or extreme fire conditions.

During the summer of 1954, I worked for several weeks with Ian Scheetel, who taught forestry at the University of Victoria. We were cruising timber in the Tumuch, Pinkerton Lake area of east-Central BC. At that time I knew that most of the trees in that area were diseased and over-mature, but there were many other places with over-mature timber that needed attention as well.

In the early 1980s nature demanded that this over-mature forest be renewed, so a spruce beetle epidemic hit that aged forest. In an effort to save as much of the wood as possible, logging roads were hurriedly pushed into the area.

The public mood was not in favour of the results of this logging, as the result was frequently touted as the cut block that could be seen from Earth orbit by the unaided eye. Several writers were extremely critical of the Ministry of Forests for allowing such a thing to happen.

Jack testing the nozzle he invented for dousing burning cedar trees. The nozzle would cool the trunk making the tree easier to fall.

During early July 1985 several different fires started in the area with the result that they finally all merged and became the Pink Fire, named because of its location near Pinkerton Creek. If memory serves me, this fire finally maxed out at about 37,000 acres. Again, the news media was critical for allowing such a horrible thing to happen, while in reality the fire was doing everyone a favour by cleaning up a horrendous mess.

Just a few years later, a fellow officer named John Currie and I did some work in that area and what we ran into was truly something to behold. We had to go through fireweed much higher than our heads, and so thick we had to bull our way through. In the three years of growth since the fire, this fireweed had laid down a cushion of humus about three inches thick. The base was laid for a new forest, and I admit I marvelled at nature's ability to heal this scar in such a short period of time. We sure understood why this plant had been named fireweed.

The point I'm trying to make is that fire is a necessary part of nature. If handled in a responsible manner there is no substitute for the benefits that can be derived from it.

Many times I assisted on slash burns, and the forces involved were awesome to contemplate. I remember reading that a 240-acre burn with medium fuel load gives off the same energy as a Hiroshima-sized atomic bomb; it just takes longer to do it. Now that public complaints about all the smoke from these slash burns has curtailed much of these burns, we need to expect a corresponding drop in wildlife.

During the 1950s Penny Spruce Mills applied for a Timber Management Licence. In preparation for what appeared to be a done deal, the company started preparing a forest development plan. I was hired along with a trapper named Sid Frank to go into a heavy stand of western red cedar trees along Slim Creek to try an experiment. As much as possible, we were to try burning these trees, which at that time were considered worthless.

With the arrival of about a foot of snow in late October, we set about torching these trees. We had a terrible time getting a fire started in many of them. Often there were no openings into the trunk area of the trees so we had to cut or chop out a place to start a fire.

It was creepy working in the area after a week or so of lighting up, because we didn't know when a tree may go down, but we persevered and kept lighting up. During the allotted three weeks we managed to get fires going in about 300 trees. Also, the Forest Service had made it clear from the outset that we had to go back to the area the following April to be certain there were no hangover fires.

April found the two of us back on site, where we discovered all fires were out. As well, we found the burning program had been

---

I must add that Frank Rapids on nearby Slim Creek was named after trapper Sid Frank. Perhaps it is worth noting that Sid was the man who told me about the huge grizzly bear that followed a portion of his trapline up Slim Creek. Sid had found the tracks of this big grizzly bear many times over the years and had noticed that it circled its line about every 10 days unless distracted by another food source.

Sid was a lucky fellow in one respect: he was cooking for a crew of river-men along the rapids on Slim Creek and while the mosquitoes were eating the others alive, he worked with his shirt off. He used to tell the other men, "If you fellows would quit slapping at them, they wouldn't bother you!"

Actually, he was just joking; his body produced a natural repellant. Oh, what I would have given for that!

a dismal failure. Less than 5 percent of the trees had burned cleanly, another 30 percent had fallen and the fires had gone out, leaving a terrible mess on the forest floor. The fires in the other 65 percent had gone out and were still standing.

Looking back at our burning effort, I am so happy that it failed, because since that time much of these old western red cedar stands are being protected and rightfully so. As the years go by it will be shown that this was indeed a wise move.

Preserving the forests

During the 1970s and '80s a lot of ancient western red cedar trees in Central BC were being cut down for lumber, and at least 90 percent of the trees were wasted because of rot-pockets. Many of the local residents in the area expressed outrage at the senseless slaughter of these old veterans and thankfully it was stopped. That ancient forest has now become a tourist's delight and is visited by a great many nature lovers every year. Trails have been cut throughout some areas and even a walkway is being provided for wheelchair access.

Aside from their beauty and unusual ecosystems, there is yet another reason for preserving many of these magnificent trees— some of this forest is estimated to be close to 1,000 years old. As well, they are home to a lot of forest creatures. How well I remember stopping in these cedar stands and pigging out on dewberries. They were so delicious that sometimes we took a bit of sugar and cream along with us. It took a bit of time to pick a bowl of these tiny jewels, but the reward was well worth it.

Probably the saddest thing I witnessed during my Forest Service tenure was the huge cut-blocks that have become so prevalent. A fellow officer joked that he spotted a caribou crossing one of these blocks and it was carrying a suitcase because it knew there would be no food for at least five miles.

When I first joined the Forest Service I thought we were there as caretaker farmers, but who ever heard of farmers killing all their newborn stock?

Memories of family life

I have many cherished memories of my folks. I can still see and hear Mom singing as she worked in her beloved garden, endlessly removing rocks from that ancient riverbed. And my father—his main love was always his horses and he spent many an hour with the curry comb in hand trying to make them look sharp. He was around horses all his life and when his health no longer allowed that to be, he let us know how much he missed them.

One of my dad's favourite sayings was: "A 15-year-old boy ran away from home because his dad was so stupid. About 10 years later he returned and was astounded by how much his dad had learned in his absence." And my mom had this to say: "This is nothing com-pared to what we had to put up with back in Saskatch-ewan when I was a child; sometimes we had nothing to live on except faith and slough water." Another of Mom's favourites was, "Raising a large family is just like being in heaven—all day and no night."

Top right: Jack's mom in her garden. Opposite: Joe Boudreau (Jack's father) with Roan and Babe.

Close call at the dam

There was a time when I could have been locked up in jail for an act that I was an accomplice to. The year was 1961, and I was employed at the mill in Upper Fraser, east of Prince George. I spent much of that summer working on the river with river-men John and Sandy Kinishy. They were an amiable couple of Japanese fellows who were moved from a prison camp to Upper Fraser during the war. They were a pleasure to work with.

Also that summer a decision was made to build a dam in a little valley about 500 yards south of the community. Its purpose was to have a head of water for the sprinkler system that was being installed in both sawmill and planer mill. This was necessary in order to bring down their enormous fire insurance costs.

The late Joe Conway was Woods Foreman at the time so he asked me to assist with the project and I willingly agreed, even though I figured it would be a challenge. We constructed the dam necessary to hold a large reservoir of water, and then proceeded with digging the six-foot deep ditch for the pipeline that was to bring the water to the mill site. We had to make certain it would be below frost level so it could not freeze during the winter months.

Everything went well until we neared the dam, where we ran into a rock wall about six feet thick which came almost up to the surface. We looked it over and finally Joe made a couple of statements I will never forget, "Sandy Kinishy has a blasting ticket but it is only good for 15 sticks of dynamite; we need at least 100 sticks to even have a chance of moving this thing."

Joe pondered the situation for a few moments and then added, "I don't have a blasting ticket so I can use as many sticks as I like; let's go!"

We went to the powder cache with a gunny sack and filled it right to the top. If I remember accurately, I think it totaled 115 sticks. We carried this bundle of dynamite back to the crime scene and dug down along the base of the rock wall; we placed the charge and covered it all up with dirt. Then, as I went one way along the road, Joe lit the fuse and quickly headed in the opposite direction. We had to make certain no person blundered into the blast area. In accordance with our plan, I hid under the hoist of a D7 cat that was stationed about 40 yards away and waited.

Suddenly the ground shook violently and then rocks could be heard falling all around me. I waited for a few minutes until the rocks that hadn't gone into orbit had all settled back to earth, and then I walked up through a monstrous cloud of dust to find Joe peering into a hole. He was laughing to the point of crying, so I followed his gaze to find that the rock ledge was completely gone. Then, still laughing, Joe pointed to a five-ton boulder that had been thrown about 30 feet from the hole. The rest of the rock was gone heaven knows where.

Were we honoured for our work? Not really. You see, there was a little matter of some broken windows down in the community, plus a number of people who had the supreme hell scared out of them. As one irate lady put it, "The very least you could have done was warn us!"

The truth of the matter is that if we had spread the word, there never would have been a blast, and all the money the company had invested in the project may have gone for naught. As for Joe, he may not have always followed proper procedure, but he sure as hell managed to get things done. He was the type of man needed for the work at hand.

Roy Sinclair: The best of friends

Sometimes in life we are blessed with an exceptional friendship, and only in retrospect do we fully realize how much that person meant to us. As a young lad, I became close friends with another lad named Roy Sinclair. Roy was one-in-a-million. He was a true friend and expected others to be the same.

One of my favourite memories of Roy was from a trip he and I and another school chum, Al, took into the mountains. We were

15 at the time and all loved the woods. Anyway, we hiked all day with our heavy packs until we came to a dry creek bed. Against Roy's advice, we made camp there, and then had to go looking for water. We started following the dry creek beds and eventually came to the stream; we got our bucket of water and then began the return trip to our campsite. All at once we were surprised to find dry creek beds running in all directions. Several times Al or I suggested one of these creek beds led to our camp; each time Roy would insist it didn't. Finally Roy insisted we follow a certain bed, and it led to our camp. Without his bush smarts, we would have spent the night without our supplies and may never have found them.

A point I must make is that all these dry creek beds were the result of a canyon washout. In one spot I recall we found a dead hollow cedar tree sticking up out of the gravel. We dropped rocks down inside it and estimated that about ten feet of gravel had built up around this eight-inch tree during its lifetime.

Anyway, this gives the reader an idea just what kind of bush smarts Roy had already learned from his father. Well known in the East Kootenays, he was the author of three novels. As well, Roy became an expert at high-lead logging, and trucking in the mountains from around the 6,000-foot level. A top-notch mechanic as well, Roy could fix and repair virtually anything. While he was still a young lad, Roy completely rebuilt a stationary diesel unit.

An explanation of the dangers faced on these narrow roads built along steep mountainsides can be attained by chatting with Roy's cousin Bob Totten of Cranbrook, BC. He was hauling logs with Roy's truck in 1970 when the edge of the narrow road gave way and he rolled down the mountain with a load of logs on the truck. By some miracle he survived, but his body took a terrible beating. As well, one of his ankles was badly smashed. After two years on crutches Bob went back to work and, surprise, surprise, he went back hauling logs off the mountains again. When I asked if he fully recovered from the leg injury, he pointed out that he still needs a cane to walk some 40 years later.

Bob Totten, was a wild man in the mountains before his injury. He followed his cougar hounds across the mountains like a man possessed. In due course Bob became quite an authority on cougars. For instance, do you know that cougars whistle? Bob raised two cougar kittens until they got to the size where he had to turn them over to a zoo. By his estimation, male cougars can weigh up to 175 pounds in the wild. Also, males can roar much the same as lions. During his 15 years of cougar hunting, Bob took a total of about 150.

Roy Sinclair filing a chainsaw the proper way so as to prevent a feather edge. Roy was a master with a chainsaw. Photo Betty Sinclair.

He recalled the time his two redbone hounds, Leo and Snarly, chased a cougar up a mountainside. Bob did his best to keep up but was unable to do so. When he finally caught up with them, the dogs had the cougar stretched out, one by the throat and the other by a hind leg. The cat was dead on his arrival.

The 175-pound weight of cougars that Bob noted applies to cats in the wild. Apparently 225-pound cougars have been taken, and although I know others who disagree with me, I suspect they were taken near habitation where they had access to easy prey and managed to put on an abnormal amount of weight.

I discussed many of Roy's stories with Bob and he assisted me with more memories. Roy spent most of his 75 years in the mountains, logging, trucking and even worked a trapline in the Flathead country south of Fernie, BC.

One adventure took place when he was hiking to some mineral claims in the mountains with his cousin Harry Totten.

Two large black bears were feeding on the slopes above them as they passed, but appeared to pay no attention to them. After they passed, the bears came down and cut their trail. Then the bears started walking after them, so the men kept glancing back and noticed the bears were gaining on them. Soon the men started running and the bears did the same. Climbing trees was not an option because the bears are far more adept at it than humans. By the time the men reached their vehicle the bears were almost upon them. Just what did the bears have in mind? Probably prospector sandwiches for lunch.

Roy had another interesting experience with wildlife. He was in the process of digging an outdoor gravity-flush outhouse at the time and when he had got to a depth where only his head was above ground level he heard the patter of little feet. He looked around just in time to see a buck deer with its antlers almost on the ground barrelling right into him. He ducked just in time, and the deer went over him and continued running away. The only sense Roy could make of it was that it was rutting season and his head bobbing up and down continually must have annoyed the animal.

James Sinclair

I can recall Roy telling me that Sinclair Pass, Canyon and Falls in Kootenay Park were named after his great-grandfather James. That's about all I knew about James until this year. I feel certain that Roy kept the truth about James a secret because few people would have believed the truth had they heard it.

James Sinclair came from good stock; his father William came to Rupert's Land (roughly Alberta, Saskatchewan, Manitoba, Hudson Bay drainage, plus the Yukon and southern Northwest Territory). He was well educated, and worked his way into the position of Chief Factor for the Hudson's Bay Company.

His son James, also well educated back in Britain, lived a life on the new frontier that made him a living legend. His life story really came to light because a researcher named D. Geneva Lent at the University of Washington spent years in pursuit of it. Given full access to the records of the Hudson's Bay Company both in Canada as well as the head office in London, England, she came out with a wealth of information about this incredible man. Her book, *West of The Mountains,* gives an insight into the harsh and unforgiving life faced by these pioneers. I quote from the preface of her book:

"Between the years 1841 and 1854, Sinclair made some daring trips across the Rockies for which he has never been given full credit or justifiable recognition. He travelled by passes never before negotiated by other than wandering Indians, including the pass that bears his name in the Rocky Mountains and the passes now known as the Whiteman Pass and Kananaskis Pass. These discoveries came about largely through Britain's need to establish, within British territory, new overland routes to the Oregon, for trade and for the protection of her valuable possessions west of the mountains."

James Sinclair pushed his luck for at least 50 years, until he was killed in a skirmish with the First Nations at The Cascades on the Columbia River in 1856. He gave his life attempting to assist others during an attack, and left a legacy of courage, pioneering, exploration and heroism that his descendants should be eternally proud of.

Eventually I spent some time working with Roy along this same Columbia River where his great-grandfather was killed. This was back in the early '50s, and more than once it was apparent to me that Roy was made of the same mettle as his great-grandfather.

One winter morning Roy and I, along with a man named Bill Oestrich, were driving to work near the river when a deer and two coyotes burst out of the woods right in front of our vehicle. One coyote had the deer by the throat, while the other was tearing its insides out on the fly. As soon as they spotted us, they quickly dove into the woods. The deer was dead, and because the coyotes were being poisoned at that time, they never returned to the kill. Some winter mornings when we arrived at our logging show the area was tramped down like a barnyard from where the coyotes chased these whitetail deer.

Ruby and Clem Rierson on Clem's 80th birthday.

I recall the Halloween when a man accused Roy of causing some damage at his place. Roy grabbed the man by the shirt and led him back to the scene. A light snow had fallen overnight and Roy forced the man to accompany him in following the tracks to their destination, where it was discovered that someone else had done the dirty deed. Roy let the fellow know in no uncertain terms never to accuse him again without proper proof.

Roy deals with a bully

An example of Roy's nature was displayed in one of his stories written before he was taken from this world by cancer in June 2008. The incident occurred during the summer of 1972 while he was employed to fall timber at Naden Harbour on what was then known as Queen Charlotte Islands, BC.

"During my five years spent falling timber along the north coast of BC, I met one man who was a real true bully, and it soon became apparent to me that I am not equipped to deal with this sort of person.

"My job was to fall the trees ahead of two shovel crews that were building right-of-way for a logging road. Once the job got underway, the crews started moving in, and with the arrival of the main crew, the swamper for the second shovel was placed in my room. This was a travesty of justice, because this guy wasn't just a drunk, or not just stoned, this guy had just crawled out of the snake pit and he figured they were still after him. I found a washbasin for him to throw up in and even emptied it for him, because the alternative would have put it on the floor. I even held him upright while he motored to the washroom and back.

"The next day I brought things from the cookhouse that I thought he might be able to keep down. All this was done incommunicado; for while he seemed to understand some of what I said, when he tried to speak it was just a slur of some foreign language. As he began to sober up, he seemed to take to me as if I was his only friend on earth. Soon he began speaking in broken English, and I learned more about his life than I wanted to know. Once fully sober, he appeared to be a decent sort and never once used a cuss word in my presence. This was rather unusual in a bush camp. I never did manage to get his name straight, so I simply referred to him as Guy.

"Guy, it turned out, was from one of the Balkan countries that NATO went to war over in the 1990s. He told me about the atrocities being carried out there: the ethnic cleansing; mass murders; bulldozed graves to bury hundreds of people at one time. He insisted he would be dead already if he had not found refuge in Canada. I didn't take him seriously at first. There, in a safe, comfortable camp at the north end of Eden Lake, it meant nothing to me, but it sure came home to roost a bit later.

"I soon got so far ahead of the shovels building the right-of-way, that I took a few weeks off and went home so the shovel crews could catch up. On my return to the camp, I was put into a different bunkhouse so I was rid of Guy, or so I thought.

"Because we ate at different times Guy didn't know I was back in camp for a while; as soon as he found out, he arrived in my room late one evening. It soon became apparent that Guy was a haunted man; terrified of something, he kept looking back toward the door or out the window. All he came for, he told me, was to warn me that 'he' would be after me too if 'he' found out that we were friends. Eventually I got the story. One of the fallers was from the same area in Europe as Guy. Unfortunately, this new fellow was from the aggressive cleanser side while Guy was from the weaker cleansed side. Once again, because of chainsaw-damaged hearing, I didn't get his name right so I just called him Butch.

"Butch acted aggressively as soon as he found out where Guy was from. First, he beat him severely, then he told Guy that every cheque had to be signed over to him; failure to do so would result in a member of his family being killed. Further, two other men of the same ethnic origin were in camp and faced with the same order. While it may seem too far out to believe, Guy was sincere and badly frightened. At that moment, as if preprogrammed, Butch stormed into my room, grabbed Guy by the front of his shirt, and pulled him off the bed where he had been sitting. He put his face close to Guy's, and shouted at him in their language. I had visions of them fighting right there in my room; blood on the floor and everything a mess. Right then something snapped inside of me. I jumped up, slashed my hand down edgewise between them, hitting Butch's wrist quite hard in the process. He let go of Guy and backed up a couple of steps looking quite surprised. I stood between them and shouted, 'Out!', and then I jabbed my pointed finger at his nose. He backed up. I jabbed again, 'Out!'

"He tried to explain that he had no argument with me but just wanted to teach Guy a lesson. It took him all the distance out of my room and halfway down the hallway to get it said, because every time he opened his mouth to speak, I would jab and shout, 'Out!'

"Heads came out of doorways but disappeared as we got close. Meanwhile, I backed him all the way down the hallway and out onto the six-foot-square plank porch. Because it is usually raining and muddy in that area, there was a network of board sidewalks between the buildings. These sidewalks were about one foot above the muddy ground. The porch had no railing, so when Butch failed to make the 90-degree turn, I backed him right off the steps. He made a most satisfactory splat in the mud, scrambled to his feet and ran as fast as he could across the mud flat to his bunkhouse; up the steps and in without looking back.

"On my way back to my room, I saw many heads being pulled back into rooms, but when I re-entered my room, there was Guy bouncing up and down in joy on the other bunk. His joy quickly faded when I pointed out that he had to pass Butch's bunkhouse on the way to his and darkness was setting in. He had a solution to that problem by getting me to stand outside until he reached his room. I did as he said, and when he passed Butch's bunkhouse he actually swaggered, the little rat.

"I was mindful that I had made an enemy, but the next morning when I went for breakfast I saw neither of them. And the same thing happened when I went for supper. That evening Guy came bouncing into my room with the news that Butch had caught a plane and was gone from camp. As there was no direct flight from camp to Vancouver, he had to fly to Masset or Prince Rupert.

"We both agreed it was good news, but that left me with a jubilant and overly grateful Guy. A few weeks later, armed with a cheque he could call his own, Guy flew out to Prince Rupert for a few days and we never saw him again.

"In retrospect, I worried about Guy for a long time, and still do. Despite being disgusted and embarrassed by the little sod, he left a mark on my memory. Did Butch really go to Vancouver, or was he waiting in Prince Rupert? Did they meet up, with Guy becoming his slave once again? My hope is that Guy got a better job and learned to stand on his own two feet.

"One thing appears certain—I am still not mentally equipped to cope with people like Butch; but then, he may not have understood anything mental."

I can relate to the thoughts that must have flashed through Butch's mind when he was confronted by Roy. Standing somewhere over six feet with the abundant muscles that come from hard work, Roy must have appeared to be a bit more than he could handle.

My favourite memory of Roy will always be his ability to throw. Not his voice, but a whistle that came from deep within his nose. He managed to fool countless people throughout his lifetime, including yours truly a few times. For instance, I recall the time he and I went by float plane to a remote lake for a few days of fishing. Just as the sound of the retreating aircraft faded away, I was surprised by the

Roy was a good friend and a talented mechanic. Photo courtesy Roy Sinclair.

sound of someone whistling in the distance in this wilderness area. Then I realized, or rather remembered that it was Roy. He was so incredibly good at it that I don't believe anyone could realize the sound originated only a few feet away unless told. One could not put a direction on the sound; it seemed to come from all around. Roy got a lot of mileage out of his strange ability throughout the years. I truly miss him because he was a good part of my life. I had some bad luck while I was in that area of the province, but Roy never once let me down. Goodbye for now, old friend.

Battle of the sexes

One evening a group of us went to a nightclub to listen to my brother-in-law play piano, at which he was extremely proficient. During the course of the evening one of my sisters asked, "Where is the women's washroom?

I immediately responded with, "First door on the corner!"

She went strutting into the room and about two seconds later came flying back out with a tremendous leap. Since she didn't go into the adjacent room, which was the women's washroom, I assumed she had already gone on the way out of the men's bathroom. Instead she returned to the table and dressed me down with, "You dirty bugger—that is the men's washroom!"

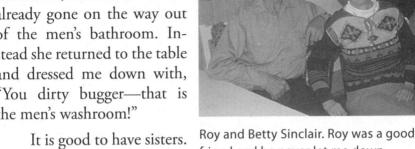

Roy and Betty Sinclair. Roy was a good friend and he never let me down.

It is good to have sisters. In fact, I have told my sisters that if I ever return to this earth I want to have 30 sisters. I don't think it would be asking too much if I stopped in for dinner at each of their homes once a month.

During my stay in a hospital, I found myself in a running battle with a nurse. We went head to toe many times until I finally figured out why I liked her: it was her sick sense of humour. One day we were having a battle of the sexes when I made the mistake of asking her, "Why do you think women are so much smarter than men?"

Instantly she came back with, "Well, because it doesn't take very much!"

Then I made an even worse mistake by asking her to give me an example.

With an obvious grin of satisfaction on her face, she replied, "Look, men spend the first nine months of their lives fighting to get out of women, and then what do they do? They spend the next 70 years trying to get back into them again—sideways; now tell me if that is intelligence!"

I had to concede that she won that round. In fact, it has been at least a year since that happened and my ego still hasn't recovered from it. You win some and you lose some.

During the years I worked for the Ministry of Forests, I tried my best to keep humour the theme of every day. Some of my jokes were met with sincere bursts of laughter, while others were met with groans. One morning I arrived at work, made coffee as usual and waited for the crew to gather. When the gang was assembled, many of the people present mentioned that they had watched a documentary the previous evening concerning muscular women. I had watched it as well, and without a doubt these women put most men to shame, muscle-wise. When asked what I thought of the documentary, I couldn't resist coming out with, "If all the women in the world looked like them, I would become a vegetarian."

My reply forced one of the women present to respond with, "That's gross, Jack. The word celibate would do."

I tried to pretend that I didn't know what the word celibate meant, but I don't think I fooled anyone.

I don't really want to, but I continually recall the day the women in the office decided to get revenge against me for perceived transgressions. They later informed me that it was all to raise money for a well-known charity. But that morning, unknown to me, they had called the police to arrest me and take me to Pine Centre Mall where I was to be locked in a cell. My only chance of escape was in the hands of the office staff, which had to raise a certain amount of money to bail me out.

Lady Luck was on my side that day, because I was called out on a wildfire just before the police arrived. After I found out about the plot, I questioned the ladies as to whether they would have bailed me out and the only answers I ever got from them was in the form of laughter. As I had to depend on them, chances are that I may still be locked in that cell, wearing a three-foot beard. Remember the saying, "Hell hath no fury like a woman scorned"?

Well, that saying just applied to one woman; try to imagine

that multiplied by a dozen women and you get the picture of the deep trouble I would have been in. As one of the ladies often put it, "We don't get mad, we just get even!"

I should have learned at an early age to be careful what I say around women. When I was about 20 years of age, I had a young lady ask me to guess how old she was. I had heard that ladies like to look younger than they really are, and as I figured she was around 18, I thought about it for a minute and then said, "About 15!"

The next thing I knew she slapped my face and shouted, "I'll have you know I'm almost 19!"

Well, as luck would have it, I was at a party only about one year later when a similar thing happened. We were talking about ages when a woman asked me how old I thought she was. Well, I wasn't going to get bit by the same dog twice, so I looked her over carefully and thought she was about 65. Remembering my former error, I eased out with, "About 80?"

"I'm only 66, you asshole!" And then I got another big slap, right on the same cheek. Now whenever someone starts talking about age, I change the subject.

A party to remember

Probably the most renowned party that occurred along the railroad line took place in the newly built home of trapper/guide Jim Hooker in the community of Dome Creek. If memory serves me right, this took place in the 1940s, shortly after the war. My mom went to their home and returned wowing and raving about their hardwood floors and what a beauty their new house was.

Well, the house was almost finished when they decided to have a housewarming party, and then all hell broke loose. Once the crowd got liquored up, the fights started, and from what I was told, went on for a good part of the night.

Our local woods-boss was a man named Steve Fowler, and he didn't mind telling us that he finally made his escape from the party and spent the remainder of the night hiding in Hooker's hay barn.

Years later, Glen Hooker described one piece of action that took place that night, "My dad got arguing with a fellow and finally went to take a mighty swing at him, but he got his arm caught in one of the support timbers and almost pulled the house down."

No doubt about it, Glen inherited his storytelling from his father, who was often depicted as a man who could tell a mean story.

Trouble on the trains: Bruce Douglas, CNR conductor

I simply have to include a story of a rather unusual man named Bruce Douglas, who was conductor for the Canadian National Railway line east of Prince George, BC. Bruce was a huge man, standing about six and a half feet tall, so he made us ordinary mortals feel quite intimidated in his presence. To make him even more intimidating, he was a boxer who fought a man named Fredrickson for the heavyweight championship of Northern BC back in the early '30s.

When asked how much he weighed, he stated, "About 365 pounds."

Tommy Wilson worked as a trainman throughout his entire life and often accompanied Bruce on trips, so he had an interesting story to add to the mix. It seems that during Bruce's time as heavyweight boxer, his father decided to make a little extra money out of his son's ability. While they stationed in Jasper, Alberta, his dad would bet $50 that no one could stay in the ring for three rounds with his son, and let's remember that $50 was a lot of money back in the '30s. Apparently it went quite well until on one occasion there happened to be a flyweight boxer in the audience. He put up his $50 and got in the ring and the two of them flew right at it. Well, I guess the little guy was so fast that Bruce couldn't catch him. He would go between his legs, out the back and by the time Bruce got turned around, he was gone. After the fight Bruce's father paid the $50 and that was the end of that venture.

In one interview with the *Prince George Citizen* on January 27, 1984, Bruce reminisced that he probably shouted "all aboar-r-r-d" a few thousand times during his 38-year stint as a railroad conductor. "I liked being the conductor be-

Bruce in the caboose of a work train. Photo Pat Armstrong.

cause I was the boss and got to meet hundreds of interesting people up and down the line," said Douglas. "When I became a conductor for the CN Railroad, I was told to clean up the passenger trains of swearing and cursing, boozing and smoking," he said, adding that "these things were never allowed on my trains."

"Many a fellow told me he'd have me fired because I poured out his whiskey, but most remained friends and later said I did them a favour," he recalled.

"Once I threw a man's cigar out and then regretted it because his feet smelled a lot worse than the cigar. When he drifted off to sleep, some of the crew took his shoes off and put deodorant in them," he chuckled.

During that interview, Bruce did not elaborate on some of the other events that transpired under his watch. For instance, there was the little matter of his walking into the caboose one day to find two of his trainmen playing hide the wiener with a married woman who resided in my hometown. The woman was thrown off the train at the next stop and didn't make her way home until the following day. Just what action was taken against the trainmen involved, I do not know, but I am prepared to bet that Bruce reported them.

On another occasion, a young man from a neighbouring town

was drunk and making an ass of himself by wandering about the car bothering people. Bruce ordered him to sit down and shut up, which he did, but a few minutes later he was at it again. Bruce stopped the train and threw him off right in the middle of nowhere in the dead of night. This man was lucky it was summertime.

When word got around that he was not one to mess with, things quieted right down on the passenger train. In other words, in a short period of time Bruce restored order to the cattle-car, as it was commonly and justifiably referred to.

And what made Bruce such a crusader for stopping drinking on trains? I'm not saying this story is true, but it is one I heard many times throughout the years. Apparently Bruce was into his share of partying on trains until on one trip the railroad had a plant on board. The story had it that he was caught drinking as well as neglecting to collect some fares, including the fare of the CNR plant who came aboard at the town of Crescent Spur. When the train arrived at the depot, Bruce was called in to face the music. The story adds that he promised, if given another chance, that he would never take another drop of alcohol. If the story rings true, he most certainly kept his word, and it becomes more understandable why he was so tough with others who wanted a drink.

I had an interesting experience with Bruce on the passenger train one night. He was sitting with his back to me about five seats away when I decided to open my suitcase as quiet as a church-mouse and share a shot or two of rum with a friend. I no sooner got the bottle open when Bruce shouted, "Okay, Boudreau, you can put that bottle away now!"

He didn't even bother to turn around, and it wasn't necessary anyway because I did like he said. To this day I do not know how he knew I had a bottle in my hands when he had his back to me. Some people have suggested that he could smell it.

Prior to Bruce bringing some law and order to the passenger trains, absolute bedlam prevailed, especially on Saturday nights. I recall the Saturday night on the cattle-car when I was seated with a friend named Oscar Mellows. Although the car was jammed full of people, it was rather quiet for a Saturday night, but that was just the calm before the storm. As soon as the train got underway things changed. Suddenly, through the thick cigarette smoke that almost occluded sight, two guys started hollering from adjacent seats. Within seconds they were up from their seats and slugging it out. Some of us began cheering them on (yes, I was guilty, too), and absolute madness ensued. As we had just arrived from the beer parlours prior to boarding the train, we did our best to cheer these would-be fighters on. Sometimes we had more fun than most people.

Anyway, when the fight got underway the conductor was in an adjoining car, probably to escape the mayhem, but he couldn't have helped even if he had wanted to. Finally a woman in a nearby seat frantically shouted to me, "Jack, get the conductor!"

So I ran into the adjoining car and slugged the conductor a couple of times.

I'm just joking, folks. Actually, when she told me to get the conductor I couldn't resist the impulse, so I shouted back to her, "Why, what did he do?"

Meanwhile, one fighter connected with a good right fist and knocked the other man to the floor. Extremely proud of himself, he shouted, "Now are you going to stop, you rooster-sucker?"

Another gentleman seated near us shouted out, "That's the first time I ever heard someone plead with a rooster-sucker to stop."

Anyway, this tough guy was standing over the guy lying on the floor of the coach with his fists clenched when another passenger shouted, "Just because his breath smells like ape-shit, he thinks he's Tarzan."

The loser of the fight crawled back to his seat and the show was over, but I can't help but wonder if perhaps this was the inspiration for the original *Gong Show*.

I also recall the time at the CNR station in Prince George when I went to get on the passenger train with a friend named Rene Michaud, both of us bound for the mill town of Penny. Rene had a case of beer in his hand and as he went to board the train, a CNR cop informed him that he could not take the beer on board. Rene didn't argue, rather he handed the case of beer to the cop with the words, "Well, here, you take it."

I scolded Rene by saying, "Don't give it to him, he'll just take it home and drink it; why not give it to Lawrence here instead?"

Lawrence Popovitch was the station agent on duty at the time, so Rene grabbed the case of beer back from the cop and gave it to Lawrence. Immediately upon taking it Lawrence said, "Wait a minute, I think I have an old suitcase inside."

He disappeared into the station for a minute and reappeared with an old suitcase. He put the case of beer into it and then handed it back to Rene. With the cop staring in disbelief, Rene boarded the train and as he passed the cop he slapped the suitcase with his hand and shouted, "Penny!"

It was my turn to board next and as I passed the cop, he gave me a withering glare of contempt; it seems he didn't approve of my actions. Perhaps I had just spoiled his party planned for that evening.

My brother Clarence was witness to some more craziness one Saturday evening when he boarded the train in Prince George. The train had not even left the station before two men, each with a case of beer, started fighting. One gentleman had the other down on a seat and was pummeling him when two CNR cops came aboard. Clarence said one cop was a huge man, really deep through the chest. Well, he walked up behind the man on top and brought his fist up into the solar plexus area with great force. The escaping air sounded much like a tire going flat, with the result that the would-be fighter collapsed and both were carried off to jail. The two cases of beer probably went off to never, never land.

On another Saturday night my brother Joe and I were on the eastbound passenger train when two men started fighting. This time the fight was over a woman, with each man professing his undying love for her. At one point the woman turned and glanced in our direction, and please believe me when I say she had a face that not even a mother could love. I'll give you two guesses whether there was booze involved, and your second guess doesn't count.

But the fun and games ended and things changed considerably after Bruce Douglas took charge of the passenger train. When word got around that he could lift a 450-pound drum of fuel to chest height and put it in a boxcar, no one wanted to challenge him in any way.

Bruce generally treated people quite well, with the result that housewives travelling to Prince George to shop often boarded with homemade pies and pastries for him. Bruce would return the favour by inviting them for coffee in the caboose.

Bruce earned the title of conductor—he started with the railroad as a patrolman in 1926. The following year he was injured quite badly in a speeder accident. He was sent to a Vancouver hospital where he spent some time in rehabilitation. Later he worked at different jobs, always returning to his first love—the railroad.

I want to end the legend of Bruce Douglas with the funniest story I ever heard concerning him, which was given to me by a member of his family. This incident occurred the day he was given two pies by a woman to repay past favours. When he rejoined his comrades with the two pies in hand they started salivating, in anticipation of sharing the wealth as usual. But as Bruce approached them he blew out a couple of monster-sized goobers and then asked, "Do any of you boys want a piece of pie?"

Green around the gills, the men shouted in unison, "No thanks!"

It would not have surprised me to learn that Bruce sat down and ate both pies before the men had time to change their minds.

After Bruce took retirement from the CNR, the passenger trains never returned to the insane craziness of the 1940s and early '50s. It was as if an era had ended. I like to think that Bruce Douglas helped send it to a timely grave.

Larry and Bernice

I love this story because it makes one realize that there are miracles in life. At least that's how it worked for Larry and Bernice Finerty. These folks owned a small ranch at Dome Creek, a tiny community about 90 miles east of Prince George, BC. Early one summer Larry needed an abundance of seed to restock his fields; trouble was he was short of cash. Reluctantly, he approached his bank, practically begging for a loan. The bank would not cooperate, constantly telling Larry, "It would be best if you used your own money."

At a loss as to his next course of action, Larry stopped at East-way Esso on his way back to the ranch. His daughter was employed in the attached store, so he bought some gas for his vehicle, then checked his pocket and found that he had just enough money left for a coffee and a one-dollar scratch and win ticket. As he sat drinking his coffee, he scratched the ticket and found that he had just won $10,000.

When Larry realized what he had won, he immediately made a phone call on the house phone. After he sat back down again, someone asked him if he had just phoned his wife. He quickly made it known that he had in fact phoned his bank. At that point he was asked, "Did you tell the bank what they could do with their non-existing loan?"

With an obvious grin of satisfaction on his face Larry replied, "Yes, but not in so many words."

Eric Davies and Skook Davidson

About a year after my book *Wild & Free* was published I received the following letter from a woman named Diane Davies Hammond:

"All my life, my father, Eric Davies, has told me stories about growing up in Prince George and the wonderful memories he has of Skook Davidson. The other night, as I was talking to my dad about a book I was reading called *Tuesday with Morrie*, my father said that the one man who had that much influence on him was Skook. My father was just a young man of 18 when he went surveying back in 1939, and had the best memories of his life, which he holds close to his heart. Skook took my father under his wing and my father has never forgotten him. I know my dad and Skook kept in contact as the years went on, and Dad has said that the most regrettable thing in his life was not saying goodbye to him before he died.

"A few years back, my father gathered the newspaper clippings and old photos from that time and made a beautiful album for my son; something he will always treasure. Now my father has macular degeneration, but I am trying to find a CD copy of your book, as this is how he now reads. I have contacted CNIB and they have put a note next to his file in case it ever comes up. Since then I have gone to the library and picked up the book, as I may have to read it to him.

"I know this may be something that is impossible, but I will ask anyway, because I will regret it if I did not. If ever you come to Langley, would it be even remotely possible for you to look up my father? I find as the years are going by that my father recollects so many events in his life from when he was a young man, and his stories I will forever hold close to my heart and pass them on to my children. Thank you so much for reading my letter and I hope to hear from you."

I had every intention of paying a visit to Eric Davies but my health problems did not allow it. Finally in 2009 I asked author Jay Sherwood if he would interview Eric. He did so in September and forwarded the finished product to me. With much thanks to Jay, I gratefully relate some of Eric's experiences in the far north of BC.

Eric began the interview by saying that his father was in love with a certain woman, but they broke up because she wouldn't leave England and come to Canada with him, so he shopped around and found one who did.

Eric's parents arrived from England in 1919, to join his brother who owned a farm in South Fort George, BC. Upon arriving, they found just a few horses and little else. The togetherness was short lived however, when the brother took to beating his horses. At that point the two families came to a parting of the way.

With little options, his parents moved into an abandoned chicken house. In short order, his mother turned it into a comfortable home. With pieces of orange boxes, they fashioned partitions and furniture; soon it was a decent living abode.

Eric was born in 1920, and he remembered his childhood as a time of freedom. He and a friend used to bicycle out to Tabor Lake where the fishing was fantastic. Every day was an adventure. The two boys would take a fry pan and a can of beans and go hiking in the woods all day without their parents worrying about them. They would carefully dig a trench taking care to cut all the roots so their campfire could not escape; life was sweet.

Eric finished high school, and spent a bit of time at the forestry camp at Aleza Lake. Then he learned that the government was hiring for the surveys in the north, and he wanted in on the action. Along with his friend Craig, they went to apply. Craig was accepted because he was a husky lad, but Eric was deemed to be too weak and skinny to cut the mustard, as the saying used to be. Eric's dad confronted them and told them not to worry about the skinny kid, because he would keep up with anyone. Eric made the crew. Then both lads went shopping: caulked boots, ground sheets, sleeping bags and mosquito dope. All the necessities needed for life in the woods.

Off they went to Summit Lake where famed Finlay River freighter Dick Corless met them. He loaded them aboard his riverboat and took off for Fort Ware.

At this point the Eric Davies interview begins:

"When we got to Deserters Canyon, Dick told us that we could not go through loaded, so we had to carry everything over the high ridge. That was when the boss, Hugh Pattinson, found out what shape I was in. I carried load after load over the ridge. When we got to Ware, Skook Davidson wasn't there yet with his horses, so we had to wait for him. We had an old cook named Addy, who could make bread or pies on an old tin stove; he was awesome.

"At Fort Ware, Craig and I went to a Native's house, and we were astounded to find dirt floors. Then we went to the chief's house and found it immaculate. We were looking for a buckskin case for Craig's camera. Chief David said to me, 'You marry my grand-daughter.'

"One of the river-men tipped off my dad about it and he joked, 'We have a room ready for you two whenever!'

"The surveyor Frank Swannell was with our party, so we went with him on a fly camp trip to meet Skook. At one of our fly camps, my feet got blistered from my new boots so they made me wait in camp while they went on to meet Skook. Finally Skook arrived with two wranglers and about 20 horses, so on we went. When we got to Sifton Pass, we started the survey work. We had to climb the highest peaks and put up rock cairns every 12 miles for the triangulation compass work. At times there was not enough available loose rock so we had to carry it quite a ways.

"We made a little cement stand to put a brass pin in, and then a number was put in the hole to identify the spot. We had to carry the cement with us, but it was just too much to carry the water for mixing the cement, so the boss would tell us to hold our pee. That was what we mixed the cement with. Swannell and I didn't get along; he didn't like me and I didn't like him. But Pattinson took me under his wing and we got along just great.

"At one site, we built up a rock cairn six feet high and sud-denly it collapsed. The air was blue with cuss words for a while after that. We'd see an old Native couple on our journey; sometimes they would come into our camps and just sit. We didn't have an abun-dance of food, so we could not feed them. At times they would point at one particular mountain and say, 'You no go there; bad!'

"The next year a crew was working up there and lightning hit the mountain, so they knew what they were talking about.

"We knew about the Bedaux expedition having gone through that country and we saw signs of their trails, but mostly we heard their horses calling to our horses. But they had gone wild by then, so we couldn't get near them.

"We had to watch for swamps, because if a horse went down

Skook loading two dead surveyors killed by lightning. Photo John Rasmussen.

in a swamp, we had a terrible time getting it out again. One day I warned Skook that there was a swamp ahead with water on it. He told me, 'No, Eric. If there's water on it, don't worry; if there's no water on it that means the water has gone down, and that's when a horse will go down.'

"We also had to watch along the river banks, because if there was a tree between the top of the bank and the river, we had to keep the horses above the tree. One time this packhorse went on the down side of a tree and it slid down into the river. The wranglers got down to it and got the pack off, and there was no damage because it was carrying canned goods. But the men could not get the horse to move; it was just frozen there. Skook shouted, 'I'll get it to move!'

"He took a rope down and passed it under the horse's tail and then brought it back up top again. He took one end of the rope and got one of the wranglers to take the other end, and then they began pulling it one way and then the other way in a sawing action. It worked. The horse just flew out of there. Skook sure knew how to handle horses.

"Once, Skook went back to Fort Ware to get supplies. He couldn't swim a stroke, you know, so he depended on his horse Big John to get him across the rivers. Well, we came to this river and Skook took a long rope across with him. The current took him and Big John down the river and he had to fight his way back upstream, but then we had a rope across the river to help us cross. One day we came upon three crosses on the bank of a river. Skook looked at them and said, 'They didn't make it!'

"We had a good summer, and spent many a night in fly camps. I always made two pine-bough beds, one for Hugh and one for myself. We would put a ground sheet over top of them and sleep in comfort.

"We worked our way right up to the Yukon Boundary, and one day we were shocked to hear voices in the woods. Suddenly out came an Alaskan survey crew. They were just as shocked to see us out there in the middle of nowhere. Five minutes earlier or later and we would have missed each other.

"For some reason Skook took a liking to me and always called me Gangly. When we were travelling he would shout, 'Gangly, get your ass up here. I want to walk for a while so you can lead the pack train.'

"I would get up on Big John and Skook would roar, 'You can't lead a pack train without a hat on!'

"So he would plunk his big black hat on my head.

"One day I told Skook that I wanted to be a banker and he roared, 'What, Gangly a banker?'

"When we were getting ready to leave, Skook gave me his hat, but I refused and left it with a note that read, 'Skook, you better keep this; you'll need it this winter to keep your head warm.'

"When we got into the riverboat to leave, he was sitting on the bank watching with his dog Jumbo. That was the last time I seen him in the North Country.

"Sometime after he got his horses back to the Kechika, Skook came to Prince George for a break. As it turned out, I had joined the air force and had just got home on leave. Skook asked, 'Has anyone heard from Gangly?'

"Someone told him, 'He's in the air force, and he's home on leave.'

"The phone rang and when I answered, a voice roared, 'Gangly, get your ass down here!'

"'Where are you?' I asked.

"'The Corning Beer Parlor. Get down here.'

"Well, it had been a long time since I had drank a beer, but I went down there and he was surrounded by hangers-on. Many people were just there to spend his money. He was buying victory bonds for the waitresses and throwing his money away. He called me aside and said, 'When I was in the army I never had enough money.'

"Skook then took out a huge roll of bills and asked me how much I wanted. I told him to keep his money. He asked when I was returning to duty and I told him I was leaving on the train at 4: 00 a.m.

"I also told him that my parents had the flu so they would not be there to see me off.

"Well I was sitting there waiting for the train, when into the station came Skook with two bags of French pastry he had bought somewhere. We walked onto the train and it was just crammed with soldiers, sailors and airmen. Skook asked me which seat I wanted, making it obvious that he would empty one for me, but I told him it was alright. He left, but he didn't take the pastry. All the folks around me gave a hand and it was devoured in no time flat."

I offer my deepest thanks to Diane for bringing her father's story to light. It is so heartening to find people treasuring and maintaining their heritage.

Clem Rierson's adventures with Skook

When folks wander around the woods, it can be advantageous to stay in a cabin when one is available. But care should always be taken to leave the cabin in the same state as one finds it; or better yet, an even better state. In one situation I became aware of, some hunters stayed in a cabin and ate up a measure of the food supplies. But most important of all, they burned up the trapper's wood supply, which was intended for his trapline use the following winter. In that instance it didn't cause any harm, because an early inspection found the problem so the wood supply and food were replenished.

Just how serious burning up a trapper's wood supply can be was demonstrated by author Clem Rierson of Enderby, BC, in his book *From Vanderhoof to Lower Post.*

Back in 1954 Clem hired on as second packer with a woodsman named Wilf Freer. Anxious for adventure, Clem's job was to help Wilf take a herd of horses into the remote Kechika River country for famed wilderness packer Skook Davidson. When the plane that was supposed to fly him back out to civilization never appeared, Clem found himself trapped in that remote area for most of the winter. It was over eight months later that Clem's family learned that he was still alive and on his way home. Perhaps because of my woods' upbringing, I rank this book up with the top 10 nonfiction books for adventure, feeling and entertainment.

During his stay of several months with Skook Davidson in the beautiful Kechika Valley, Clem recorded many stories that were related to him by the master woodsman.

A story from the book that caught my attention got underway when Skook told Clem about travelling 25 miles on snowshoes to Netson Lake to visit a trapper friend. This friend had stopped at Skook's ranch a month earlier during a period of bitterly cold weather, so Skook was concerned about his welfare. The weather had recently warmed, which made it a good time to check on his friend, so Skook headed for the trapper's main cabin.

"Well, when I got close enough to see the shack," Skook said, "there was no smoke coming out of the chimney, so I thought the old fellow must be out in one of his line shacks. As I got closer I noticed the door wasn't quite shut. When I went in, there he lay frozen on the floor and not a piece of kindling or shavings in sight. The poor fellow must have been extremely cold, and near exhaustion before he got to his shack. Someone had been there, more than likely the previous summer, and burned the wood supply and had not the intelligence to cut any kindling or restore the wood."

Skook continued, "The trapper must have been just too cold to get a fire going because his axe, knife and a few burned-out matches lay on the floor by the heater with some branches and twigs that he managed to scrounge up to get a fire going. Anyway, he must have been just too cold to get the fire started and succumbed right there."

It was, as Clem points out in his book, the unwritten law of the north that people always left a cabin in the condition in which they found it. Failure to do so had cost this man his life.

Clem's book is full of constant adventure and forces the reader to accept the superb conditioning and toughness of the First Nations people back 60 years in time. It illustrates what they endured when they were forced to live off the fruits of an often merciless and unforgiving wilderness existence. For instance, during their mid-winter 100-mile trek out to Lower Post, they never saw one animal that they could shoot for food; they only managed to shoot a few grouse.

Try to imagine Clem and Wilf snowshoeing through that wilderness in sub-zero temperatures and meeting a Native squirrel hunter out there alone with his dog. That man was Jack George, aka Eagle Eye, because of his outstanding eyesight. Though he was at least 60 miles from the nearest habitation, Jack was travelling light and appeared totally unconcerned. After he asked if they had any moose meat with them, they told him that there was some moose meat left at a cabin in the Kechika Valley. Then Jack continued on his way still further from civilization. He also stated that he may visit Skook in the Kechika Valley, which would put him 120 miles distant from his home in Lower Post. He further added that he intended to carry on to Moodie Creek to trap, which would have put him roughly 100 miles from home.

The bare existence available to the First Nations people, especially away from coastal areas, was extremely difficult and often starvation was a constant companion. And all the more so for those without access to salmon; when berry crops failed, food was exceedingly hard to come by. As I learned from the Kechika guide Frank Cooke, Starvation Flats south of the Yukon Boundary came by its name honestly.

Skook and the elusive sasquatch

There are another few stories Clem coaxed out of Skook that I find extremely interesting; they concern the sasquatch or mountain men as they are sometimes referred to. A few years earlier, or about mid-summer 1952, Skook had taken two Native guides with him on an exploration trip, intending to visit the headwaters of the Gataga River. He wanted to check the feasibility of taking a hunting party in there. Skook told Clem, "We only rode upriver one day and these fellows got very uneasy and refused to go any farther. They were superstitious and scared stiff and said, "Big hairy tings, walk standing up, no-go, no-farther."

The two guides quit the trip and rode back to the ranch. Skook continued on alone, and had some curious experiences when something or things kept looking out through the trees and watching him around his campfire. Although he repeatedly saw the reflection of eyes, he never determined what it was.

Let's take note that these two guides were born and raised in the woods and knew all the animals that dwelt therein. This adds a great deal of credibility to these stories.

Similarly, Skook took another Native guide with him on a trip while the man's wife stayed and waited at his Diamond J Ranch. When the two men returned, they found the door nailed shut and furniture piled up against it to prevent entry. Skook finally kicked in the door and they found the woman under a bunk in a state of shock. After she came around she told how she had watched a giant hairy being without clothes walking upright in the bright moonlight. It was on the hillside above the ranch and continually looked down in her direction. Take note that this creature was out in the moonlight; does this suggest, as some people state, that these creatures are mostly nocturnal?

Also worth mentioning is the fact that this woman was raised in the woods and would have known all the wildlife in the area. Certainly this has to make her reactions all the more reasonable and understandable. Native folklore contains countless stories of these hairy beasts taking Native women as their own.

I have yet another story from a man who has worked in remote areas of BC for many years. His story started with five young men, one of them named Aaron, leaving Prince Rupert in 1998 to explore the Rainbow Lake area. They worked their way along a few little lakes and then into Rainbow Lake. In need of something to eat, they stopped at a guide's cabin and filled their faces, as the saying goes. Then Aaron and one other man hiked out to get their vehicle while the others rowed across the lake. During that time the men were shouting "Wiiget, Wiiget!" They had been told by the Natives that these creatures were called Wiiget in their language.

When Aaron and his partner returned with the vehicle, their friends were nowhere to be seen. Finally their friends came out of the woods in varied states of shock. Just after the two had left, they had been attacked by something throwing rocks at them. But these were not rocks that a human could throw; these were huge rocks. The men had huddled in fear, hiding behind rocks or trees, unable to retreat because there was just the lake behind them and it was getting dark. Once they got back to the vehicle, they could not get out of the area fast enough.

I had a long, interesting talk with Lee Milnes of Prince Rupert, BC. He was one of the men assailed by the creature in the woods. He assured me that it was a harrowing experience that he would not care to endure again. Both men I talked with suggested the possibility that calling out their names could have played a part in their experience.

A short time after the episode at Rainbow Lake, Lee told Aaron, and later myself, that he had been canoeing up the coast and as he got near shore, something began throwing large rocks at him. Then a tremendous scream seemed to come at him from above, rather than from the shore. He never got a clear look at the creature(s) in the woods, but he thought he saw small legs running behind some bushes, possibly indicating a family. He also stated that one should never call their name, "Wiiget."

The reason so many people, including myself, have found the entire Bigfoot controversy hard to accept, is because there appears to be no physical evidence. Where are the skeletons? Most important to me, is where do they spend the winters? Are they nocturnal? If so, that would explain the inability to get clear photographic proof. I never attached any importance to these stories because after glassing the mountains for over 50 years, we never spotted any of these beings. In retrospect, we lived in a high snowfall area with about seven months of winter. Any attempt by these creatures to live there would no doubt result in the same fate the wild horses suffered—starvation.

So just where should these beings reside? We only have to study maps of the reported sightings and it becomes apparent that most are clustered relatively near Pacific coastal areas.

Perhaps this answers the question of why so many Native people in different places along the coast have attested to the existence of these monster beings. So sasquatch hunters, here is a good lead for you—stop searching for these creatures in New York State or London, England, and head into remote areas. According to Skook, the upper Gataga area is a low-snowfall region which should be a choice site for these beings, if they exist. Further, the milky waters of the Gataga River show that it is fed by glacial water, and glaciers provide a constant source of water for life forms during dry summers.

Since I wrote my opinion about the sasquatch phenomenon being a hoax, I have had several people insist that I was on the wrong track. Understandably, the biggest problem is that people are reluctant to come forward stating that they have seen these creatures but can't prove it. And let's face it, what would stand up as proof?

What really made me take another look at this phenomenon was when I found out that my lifelong friend, Roy Sinclair, had experienced an encounter. First off, I state straight out that Roy was one of the most honest and sincere people I have ever known. He spent his life in the mountains of the East Kootenays and knew all the wildlife therein.

Early one morning while it was still dark, Roy was driving to work when he met two adult sasquatch members standing right beside the road. He slammed on the brakes, but by then he had gone past them. He put the truck in reverse and quickly backed up, but they had melted into the forest.

If these creatures do exist as so many people swear they do, there is a potential story here that could blow the roof off conventional knowledge.

Another good lead for sasquatch hunters concerns an incident that occurred last year. A man was pushing a new development road for logging into a remote mountainous area near Stewart, BC, when he experienced an encounter. It was just after daybreak and he was driving to where his crawler tractor had been left, when he drove right up to a huge hairy bipedal beast. It was standing right in the ditch beside the road with an armload of skunk cabbage and stared right at him for a moment before it turned and ran away. This individual swears that the creature appeared to be close to 12 feet tall and was all covered in white hair. Make of this what you will, but the uncle of this driver assured us that this man is being truthful and that he was freaked right out by the incident. Understandably, this Cat operator refuses to be interviewed. But once again it suggests that these creatures frequent the most remote areas of the wilderness, if they do exist as many people swear they do.

One need only go online to learn that Bigfoot encounters have gone on for centuries. As well, their relatives are on most continents. The sherpa men who frequent the Himalayan mountains insist they do exist.

On different occasions sailors along our Pacific coast have been freaked out by them. In one incident a sailor fired his musket at one and his gun exploded in his face. As far as I can determine, Daniel Boone claimed to have shot one, but that should be taken with a grain of salt because he produced no evidence. Also, one of the world's most celebrated mountaineers, Reinhold Messner, claimed he shot one when they met face to face in 1986.

Back in 1884 during the construction of the Canadian Pacific Railway, a young "Wildman or Sasquatch" was taken into captivity near Yale, BC. I am not certain of how the story ended, but if memory serves me right, I believe it died in captivity.

Alexander the Great is said to have captured one during their trek across the Himalayas back in 326 A.D., but let it go free when the natives told him it could not survive at lower elevations.

In her book *Canadian Folklore,* published in 1913, Edith Fowke mentions the sasquatch: "Canadians also tell many stories about the Sasquatch, the Canadian version of the monster known elsewhere as Bigfoot, the Abominable Snowman, or the Yeti. Hundreds of witnesses have reported seeing a monster who conforms to the sasquatch concept—a huge animal-type being who walks like a man—and many of the accounts are detailed and convincing. But most scientists remain skeptical, and it appears that the Sasquatch will not move from the field of legend to that of historical truth until one is produced either dead or alive."

It is not easy to dismiss the claims of men such as David Thompson (Thompson River). He was one of our most famous explorers, fur traders and geographers. On January 7, 1811, he attempted to cross the Rocky Mountains near the present-day site of Jasper, Alberta. In his journal he wrote:

"I saw the track of a large animal – has 4 large toes about 3 or 4 in. long and a small nail at the end of each... The whole is about 14 in. long by 8 in. wide & very much resembles a large bear's track. It was in the rivulet in about 6 in. of snow."

The following year Thompson recounted the experience. "I now recur to what I have already noticed in the early part of last winter, when proceeding up the Athabasca River to cross the mountains, in company with some men and four hunters, on one of the channels of the river, we came to the track of a large animal, which measured fourteen inches in length by eight inches in breadth by a tape line." Because the snow was around six inches deep, the monstrous track was easily spotted one hundred yards ahead of him and his crew. He was traveling with four hunters, and Thompson noted that regardless of the hunter's eager desire to follow the track of any animal in hopes of a kill, no one dared to follow this beastly one. He wondered what damage their fowling guns could actually do to such an animal. Thompson was familiar with many tales of large animals from men living in the area, but always considered the stories to be folklore or myth. "Report from old times had made the head branches of this river, and the mountains in the vicinity the abode of one, or more, very large animals, to which I never appeared to give credence; for these reports appeared to arise from that fondness for the marvelous so common to mankind." He admits however that the track he saw truly mystified him, and he could never bring himself to believe an animal of that size existed. He thought that it could possibly be the track of some "monster bear."

Forty years later Thomson added a bit to the experience:

"January 7th continuing our journey in the afternoon we came on the track of a large animal, the snow about six inches deep on the ice. I measured it; four large toes each of four inches in length, to each a short claw; the ball of the foot sunk three inches lower than the toes. The hinder part of the foot did not mark well, the length fourteen inches by eight inches in breadth, walking from north to south, and having passed about six hours. We were in no humour to follow him; the men and Indians would have it to be a young mammouth [mammoth] and I held it to be the track of a large old grizzly bear; yet the shortness of the nails, the ball of the foot, and its great size was not that of a bear, otherwise that of a very large old bear, his claws worn away, the Indians would not allow."[1]

1.   J.B. Tyrell, ed., *David Thompson's Narrative of his Explorations in Western America 1784-1812* (Toronto: The Champlain Society, 1916), 10.3138/9781442618114.

It becomes instantly apparent that this was not a bear. Bears do not have four toes. They have small toes, not four inches long, and grizzly claw marks fall far ahead of the front paw tracks even after a summer of digging. Take note that he only mentions one size of track; this seems to indicate a bipedal creature as opposed to one walking on four legs. Also, Thompson's First Nations guides would not follow it. As was the story with Native people throughout their known history, they would not follow these creatures. This begs the question of how such respect was born. Take note how Thompson's thoughts continually reverted to this creature— he knew it was something unusual.

Several noted mountaineers sent expeditions to the Himalayas in search of the fabled yeti, but to no avail. Perhaps the most noted was the Sir Edmund Hillary attempt during 1960–61. As far as I can tell, these groups spent their time searching around the 17,000- to 18,000-foot level. Since it is unlikely that these creatures live on ice or snow, someday a group should try searching down lower in the forests where their food has to be.

There must be a message in the fact that these creatures are familiar to Native people all over the world. The story of Zana, an Almas female claimed to have borne four human-Almas babies in the Caucasus region bears further scrutiny. The offspring could speak although they were a bit erratic and hot tempered.

The *Sunday Journal and Star* in Lincoln, Nebraska, carried the following headline in its July 29, 1934, issue:

ARE THEY THE LAST CAVE MEN? BRITISH COLUMBIA STARTLED BY THE APPEARANCE OF "SASQUATCH"—A STRANGE RACE OF HAIRY GIANTS.

The cover carried a drawing of a huge beast throwing rocks at a First Nations person in a canoe, forcing him to withdraw from a salmon fishing stream. Over and over this theme of throwing huge rocks at intruders is repeated.

The number of sightings throughout the centuries is astronomical, and if even 5 percent of the reported sasquatch encounters are real, this constitutes an astounding abundance of evidence. And let's remember that, as in the previous encounter by the Cat operator, many encounters are not reported because people are certain they will be subjected to ridicule. As things stand at the moment, I guess I have to see them for myself to be convinced. But what good would that do if I kept it to myself?

The October 17, 2013, edition of the *Calgary Herald* newspaper carried a story about the research of Oxford University's geneticist Bryan Sykes. He compared two different hair samples—one found in the upper western Himalayan region of Ladakh in Northern India, and the other in Bhutan, 800 miles east—to be a perfect match to a bear that lived 40,000 to 100,000 years ago.

This ancient bear was found in Svalbard, Norway, and existed before the polar bear and the brown bear had separated as two different species. The hair sample from Ladakh was preserved by the hunter who shot the bear 40 years ago. The hunter found the animal to be so unique and alarming, he kept some of the remains. The second sample from Bhutan was preserved by an expedition of filmmakers, who found the hair in a bamboo forest 10 years ago.

Sykes pointed out that this species of bear has not been recorded for 40,000 years, yet now there's proof that there was one walking around 10 years ago, and another, at the other end of the Himalayas, 30 years previous. He is certain that if someone were to search for the species on the Himalayas today, it could be found.

Sykes' research, which has been submitted for publication in a peer-reviewed science journal, will feature in a new British documentary series, *Bigfoot Files*.

Prospecting in BC

Many prospectors have had interesting experiences while looking for the motherlode. Freda and Bert Allan are a good example. One summer they left their claim just south of Cottonwood House, BC, to do some prospecting at Sandon in the West Kootenays. Two months later they returned and learned that their watchman had discovered that someone had been high-grading in their pit.

The watchman had not seen him because he had dug a little tunnel just out of sight by lying in muddy water. They did manage to get the licence plate, which they reported to the police. The policeman asked, "How deep can that machine dig?"

They replied, "Twenty-six feet."

The policeman came back with, "Well, that's where you should put him if you ever see catch him here again."

I never did find out if they obeyed the police directive because they were too evasive on the subject.

Cariboo Jack and Old Potatoes

One thing I admire about prospectors is their eternal optimism. They also have a fortitude that defies logic. How about the Chinese miner Wong Man Ding, also known as Cariboo Jack? He walked all the way up the Cariboo Highway from Yale to 150-Mile house, then to Quesnel Forks, over the mountains to the Swift River and eventually to Stanley. He prospected in that area for 50 years and only left the area once, which was to Prince George where he spent the winter with a Chinese hooker nicknamed "Old Potatoes." That spring she moved back to Stanley with him where she stayed until her death in 1928. Hers is the only Chinese grave left in the Stanley cemetery. Soon after her death Jack returned to China where he passed away two years later.

There are so many wonderful stories about the Barkerville gold rush; some stories relate unbearable hardships and some stories lift a person's spirits, such as the three Chinese miners who found one nugget big enough to pay their return trip to China for a visit.

The above two stories are just a small sample of what awaits the reader of W.M. Hong's book, *And So That's How it Happened*. This book contains countless stories about the towns of Barkerville, Stanley and nearby Van Winkle, mostly from 1900 on. Van Winkle, which had a population of about 500 people at one time, was deliberately burned down in 1910 to make way for tailings. But prior to that time, Barkerville already had established itself as one of the richest gold strikes in history.

Empty graves

During the month of June 2011, Dave Humphreys, of Prince George, and I went on a trip toward Barkerville, BC. When we arrived at the ghost town of Stanley, we took a tour down a side road where we were met by a lot of empty graves. At first glance one could assume that grave robbers had been at work there, and in a sense they had been. I don't mind stating that it gave me a weird feeling seeing those empty graves, but then Dave had already pointed out to me that these graves had been dug up and the bones from there, as well as from nearby Barkerville, had been returned to China many years earlier.

A nearby sign noted:

Gold was discovered in nearby Lilamine Creek in 1861 resulting in the towns of Likely and Van Winkle springing up; this hill-top cemetery probably came into being soon after. Here lies Harry Jones, a beloved Cariboo pioneer. Beside him is buried Captain John Evans, leader of 26 Welsh miners "The Welsh Adventurers."

The open pits of 36 Chinese graves, many of which have sloughed in during the intervening years, indicate that the graves were dug up long ago. The bones were dug up, identified, dried, placed in bags and shipped to Victoria; then Hong Kong, and finally distributed for burial in the family plots in China. The Chinese Hospital Association in Victoria was in charge of looking after the details of the move.

I was certainly surprised to learn that the Chinese had been buried in separate gravesites from the Occidentals because of this habit of digging up the graves at least 10 years after burial and returning the remains to China.

Although this Chinese custom may seem strange to us, in their culture it obviously carries great significance. Perhaps we can learn a lot from them about caring for our own pioneers, as well as their traditions.

Barkerville has an awesome history, from being burned out to having unsolved murders.

Fortunes made and fortunes spent; it has it all. One individual made money by digging up the ground for gold after places were burned by fires; who knows, perhaps he caused some of the fires. If so, he only had to dig up the surface of the ground, compared to the other prospectors who often had to dig deep for their gold.

One of the most intriguing stories ever to come to my attention concerned a trapper and prospector named Ben Miller. Ben worked the Quesnel River area for most of his lifetime, and because of a favour he did for a friend, it was a life lived alone. As a young man, Ben chummed around with a fellow who had several encounters with the law. One day the friend was charged with theft, which meant that he expected to do a long stint in prison. He begged Ben to take the rap for him, stating that because he had a clean record, he would get off with a slap on the wrist. He also added that because he was engaged, his fiancé would definitely break it off if he were to go to prison.

Ever the good and trusting friend, Ben bought the story, and even though he was going with a girl that he deeply cared for at the time, he pleaded guilty to the charge. The end result of his kind act was that he spent five years in prison, less time off for good behaviour.

The Kelowna emerald

The following story has taken so many twists and turns that I have scarcely been able to keep up with it. For me, this story really started when I received a phone call from my nephew David Humphreys. At that time he was in Kelowna BC, holding what the newspapers described as the world's largest cut-faceted emerald. Was David excited, you ask? You bet he was, and he filled me in with what he knew at that time. Next he sent me an e-mail picture of himself holding the emerald.

Auctioneer Mike Odenbach was in possession of the emerald, which went up for auction in Kelowna, with an opening bottom price of $500,000. No one bid on what some people estimated was a $2 million gem. What was the problem?

The owner of the emerald was a gem buyer named Regan Reaney from Calgary, Alberta, who claimed the gem was found in Brazil and had been sent to India for cutting, where he had purchased it. He claimed it was named Teodora, which in Greek means "Gift from God." What led credence to the value of the gem was a gemologist named Jeff Nechka, who valued the stone at well over a million dollars. Even though Reaney had admitted to adding dye to the gem, Nechka pointed out, "If it was white (beryl) that was dyed green, it would be a lot more even in color and would be lighter in tone."

One must take notice that the owner and the gemologist both resided in Calgary, although the attentive media did not push that point.

News of this stupendous find flashed around the world and drew more attention than perhaps had ever been expected. Soon the plot thickened, as the saying goes. It wasn't long until a Vancouver man, Chris Dirken, stated that he had been bargaining on E-bay with the seller of this same stone and had tried to get it for a couple hundred dollars. The seller then informed him that he had received a higher bid, so the deal fell through.

Once the media got involved, all hell broke loose. *The Globe and Mail* pointed out, "Emeralds are easily faked by dyeing common white beryl mineral green."

Soon a heavyweight entered the fray in the form of Shane Mc-Clure, director of the west coast identification services at the Gemological Institute of America in Carlsbad, California. He pointed out that white beryl is almost worthless, and then stated, "White beryl could be dyed any color or intensity you wanted. If the gemologist says it has been dyed, there's no way to know how much dye has been used. It is not a difficult thing to take a large chunk of opaque beryl and dye it green and call it an emerald. Beryl like that is easily available in huge pieces. Beryl pieces 20 feet long have been found."

The plot thickened even more when the RCMP arrested Reaney on an outstanding warrant issued at Hamilton, Ontario The charges allegedly included four counts of false pretenses and two counts of fraud under $5,000. Consequently, when the emerald went up for auction in Kamloops, no one bid.

And so, that's where it sits. Whether some person will chance the gamble of purchasing it remains to be seen. Shane McClure makes it plain that he would not touch it.

Confederate treasure

Sometimes it seems that people are destined to walk into odd adventures, and such was the case with Stan Bergunder of Quesnel, BC. In his case, he walked into the same sort of situation twice. In my entire lifetime I have never seen Confederate money, but let's take a look at what happened to Stan.

While at an auction, Stan threw in a bid on an old suitcase. When he opened it, he found a bunch of Confederate money. Just how legitimate the bills may be is open to question, because several equal value bills have the same serial number.

The real kicker, though, occurred while Stan was running a line on one of his mineral claims near the Willow River. As he moved through the forest he came upon the remains of an old tumbled-down cabin that had been erected many years earlier. Suddenly he looked down to find a rusted-out tobacco can directly in his line of travel. He gave the can a kick and realized there was something inside of it. He opened the can to find about one dozen confederate bills.

It is anyone's guess just how long the money had been there. If the rusted-out can had been dragged from the cabin by an animal, it could have been there for over a century. We've heard the saying, "Phony as a three-dollar bill." Well, in among the bills was a three-dollar bill printed in the Republic of Texas. Also an eight-dollar bill printed in New York dated 1776. Another ten-dollar New York bill which contained the words, "Tis death to counterfeit."

All of the eight bills found in the trunk were printed on one side only, while the twenty bills found in the can had the value printed on the back side of the bills. An eight-dollar bill had "State of Maffachufetts" printed across the top, while in the small print was the proper spelling of the state. It smells rather strange to me and that could mean it is rotten.

· Stan had another interesting story to tell from years gone by. A trapper/miner asked him to install a 100-gallon propane tank at his cabin to run his fridge, lights, etc. Stan convinced the man that he needed much more than 100 gallons and instead installed a 1,000-gallon tank. Through the years the two men became close friends. Many years later the miner became ill and was taken to the Quesnel Hospital where Stan called to visit. Near death, the miner told Stan to contact his daughter in Vancouver and give her his money and gold, which Stan would find under the fridge in his cabin.

Stan went to the cabin and moved the fridge, but all he found was a pile of moss, which he thought was a pack rat's nest. He gave the moss a kick and discovered a hole in the floor. Inside the hole he found three Vogue tobacco cans. One contained cash, another held over half a can of fine gold, and the third was over half full of coarse gold. This was a pretty substantial amount of money when converted to cash.

Stan immediately called the daughter in Vancouver, who must have left right away because she arrived the next morning. She was given the three cans with their contents and told to square up with the funeral costs and other bills her dad's death incurred. A few days later Stan was contacted by the funeral home and told that he had to pay the costs. It seems that the daughter had grabbed the money and ran. Stan phoned the daughter in Vancouver but she refused to pay anything and told Stan he could do whatever he wanted with the body because her dad had ran off on them years earlier. She flatly refused to pay anything. The end result was that the taxpayers paid all the costs and Stan was the only person to attend the funeral. Go figure!

Photo Dusty Palmer.

PART THREE

THE MYTH OF LIVING PEACEFULLY WITH PREDATORS

Over the years my own experiences and those of the guides and woodsmen I have known all point to the need to deal with the increase in grizzly numbers by also increasing hunting quotas. In order for us to be able to share the land with bears there must be constant and honest accounting of the bear numbers.

As well, I must state that a growing problem in BC is the increased aggressiveness of grizzlies in some areas. Over and over we learn that hunters are being chased off their game by grizzlies. In many cases grizzlies are coming directly to the kills when they hear gunshots, or following hunters to their camps and stealing their game.

A wildlife officer in Yellowstone Park summed it up this way: "There is going to be a response from ranchers and hunters in that they are going to take the approach of, 'Shoot, shovel and shut up!'"

Surely we are heading into the same situation in parts of British Columbia. In fact, I have every reason to believe it is happening at this time. I think having protected bears in certain areas started this problem to begin with, and so-called bear experts mingling with grizzlies along salmon streams has exacerbated the problem. We now have to accept the fact that in many areas grizzlies have lost their fear of humans. Just how or if it can be dealt with at this point is the question. Perhaps it is too late.

In Yellowstone, they cannot allow hunting in areas where tourists are visiting each year, even if the parks are closed during that period of time. The major worry in allowing hunting in parks is having tourists walking in areas where wounded grizzlies could lie in wait. This idea doesn't fly.

One of the major problems in my view is that there are far too many "bear experts," yet many of these people hardly spend any time in the woods. Some of these experts can't seem to agree on anything and understandably so. Here's the main reason why:

During the many years I spent interviewing retired woodsmen I have had one overriding fear—that one day two of them would agree on everything, because then I would know the end of the world was at hand.

Here's one example:

When I was a lad of 13, three members of my family were heading into the mountains so I begged and pleaded to join them. On our second evening we were sitting by a campfire in the subalpine when we spotted a cougar walking across a snowfield high above us. When we returned home a sports day was in progress in the community. Present was an old-time trapper named Jack Evans who trapped the area north of Prince George before 1900. As Jack was my namesake and a renowned woodsman, I had tremendous respect for him. We approached him and told how we had seen a cougar on the mountain, but he let us know straightaway that we were mistaken. We insisted, even mentioning the long tail, but he shook his head in the negative. He then informed us that he had spent his entire life in the woods and had never seen a cougar.

The message is that we are all prisoners of our own experiences. Since we have different experiences, how can we agree?

For that reason, one man's bear expert can be another man's fool. Besides, even if one is a bear expert, if one is not a wildlife expert as well, what is the point? To endlessly promote the predators at the expense of the ungulates is counter-productive.

How is it possible that studies can be done in an area and the results show that grizzly bears are in trouble when locals and guides claim there are too many bears?

I must relate a story told to me by a retired guide. He said a man of the cloth told him, "It says in the Bible that man shall live in peace with wild animals, so it is time to get on with it."

That very night this guide had a dream in which that same man of the cloth was addressing a gathering of bears. He heard him shout, "I am prepared to give up the three evils if all of you will stop eating flesh! Well, why are you silent? Why are you all looking at me like that? Wait! Stop! Don't come any closer! Stop! Stop it! Heeellllpp!"

Was that a bit morbid? It's not my fault—the bear experts have driven me to this end.

Seriously, though, I know of one instance where a young man was sent into a remote area to do grizzly studies. He set up headquarters in a subalpine valley that was seldom visited by grizzlies and even when they did visit that area it was at a different time of year. This was during August when the grizzlies were down on the salmon streams and in the berry thickets at lower elevations.

On top of that, he tramped around the area, so being that these grizzlies were extremely *wild* at that time, they would have left or gone into seclusion as soon as they learned of his presence. Does it not follow that his report suggested that although he found old hair and scat samples, the grizzlies appeared to be at the point of extinction in there?

Here's another example—when we first began finding large numbers of grizzlies around Grizzly Bear Mountain, just six miles away was Sam Driscoll Ridge, which extends up near timberline. I spent two weeks running fire pumps there and had lots of time to explore between pump fill-ups. I explored the ridge thoroughly and found not a trace of grizzly sign, diggings, or even old scat samples. Just picture someone doing studies up there.

I could go on, but I do not want to find fault with the people doing the studies; I'm sure they all do their very best. Besides, we can have all the studies we want, but to expect bears to survive where there is little or no food will always end in failure.

During my many years studying grizzlies around timberline, I learned just how clever they are. If we walked through a certain valley, the bears were gone the next day. They would reappear after we left the area, but they would re-enter the area at night. If our scent was present, they would not be there the following day. Most hikers have no comprehension how much game they drive away or into seclusion.

It strikes me that there are two opposing forces at work here. There are the people who live out in the woods, and there are people who are dreamers. Some folks would have us live side by side with these bears in peace as long as their families are safe. I can't speak for others, but I don't want the bears eating my grandchildren.

Grizzlies were believed to be at the edge of extinction in Alberta a few decades back, as an article in the *Prince George Citizen* pointed out on August 17, 1981. A grizzly bear specialist named Rick Langshaw noted the impending demise of the grizzly bear. "The population levels are already at critical levels; I'm convinced that the population will be wiped out in one to two decades."

Well, three decades have passed and the bears are still…or are they? What are the experts saying now? Are the grizzly bears still a threatened species?

On May 2, 2013, the *Calgary Herald* carried headlines concerning this exact situation. Kevin Van Tighem, a former superintendent of Banff National Park, stated that in order to protect the threatened species in the province, Albertans need to learn to live with grizzlies and stop being afraid of them. He argues that the "keep-bears-scared-of-people paradigm" will be nothing but harmful to the bears, and we need to learn to manage them without fear.

"…The strategies are all part of the Grizzly Bear Recovery Plan 2008–2013, which was implemented after studies found there were fewer than 700 grizzly bears in the province—a number that led to their status as a threatened species."

The 1,012-pound cattle-killer; try living with him if you are a rancher. Ministry of Environment photo.

First off, I'll bet there are no bears on his block threatening his home or family. Next, I suggest he look into the huge grizzly that was living on beef near Houston, BC. It is mounted and on display in the Smithers Airport.

Roger Britton Sr. and Jr. have owned their taxidermy shop in Smithers, BC, for 35 years, during which time they have seen it all. For many years they had a sign in their shop that read, "We will full mount for free any grizzly that squares over nine feet."

When wildlife officers finally got this grizzly it weighed out at 1,012 pounds. This beast squared out at nine feet one and a half inches. Imagine a bear with a seven-inch pad attaining that size and weight. The one thing Roger and I disagree on is this—he feels this is a genetic thing and that there are more bears that size in the area. Perhaps that is because another bear almost as big was taken since the first one. I feel that the size of the pads gives away the fact that these bears didn't have to work for a living. They just walked out and killed beef whenever they so desired and this was evident in their increased sizes and weights.

Regardless, the Anderson ranch at Hungry Hill was missing a good many cattle. But the problem was not over after these bears were shot, because soon another bear invited itself to a beef smor-gasbord. So it appears there will still be a lot of munching at the rancher's expense.

As for the "learn to live with them," I suggest Van Tighem talk to the relatives of the people killed and eaten in Yellowstone Park recently, or the Huffman family for that matter.

Perhaps we should listen to the people spending their lives in the woods when they tell us there are too many bears already. Wouldn't it be nice if instead of talking down to them, we listened up for a change? There's a lot to be learned there.

Is Kevin Van Tighem correct that grizzlies are a threatened spe-cies in Alberta?

The Willmore Wilderness Foundation survey has some insight on this subject.

Grizzly bear survey

"In April 2008 and after a lot of thought, the Wilmore Wilderness Foundation decided to gather as much grizzly bear information from traditional sources as we could. This Grizzly Bear Survey would be used to supplement the data gathered by the foothills Research In-stitute.

"We requested that our members and other groups who spent considerable time on the eastern slopes and in the foothills regions forward any sightings of grizzly bears. We hoped to glean as much information as possible: i.e. colour; sows with cubs; age of cubs; whether the bears were alone or with a group; the bears' activities; and whether there were collars or ear tags. Individual traditional land users forwarded their information to [the above address.]

"The foundation had three persons on staff that took the sight-ings information and created a database, which included detailed descriptions, some GPS locations of bears, photographs and con-tact information of every report for further follow-up. After eight months of collecting data, we had close to 500 bear sightings and dozens of reports of tracks where the bears were not seen. Most of the sightings were from Highway 16 north; however, there were some from as far south as the Montana border.

"Our statistics included the fact that there had been three grizzly attacks west of Calgary over the past twelve months, which resulted in two deaths. This spring one oil and gas sector worker was mauled in the Kakwa Region by a grizzly. We also had a report from a former Alberta Forest Service Ranger that his horse was killed by a grizzly just west of Edson. We had numerous reports from oil field workers that grizzlies were seen well east of their usual habitat. One grizzly bear was live-trapped near the schoolyard in Susa Creek, a remote community near Grande Cache. We also received reports of grizzly sightings on other Native Co-ops near Grande Cache where children play. One Grande Cache man reported that a grizzly charged his truck, while a local woman described how a grizzly bear charged her car. Biologists from the University of Laval have been doing goat studies on Caw Ridge for the past fifteen years and have seen a steady increase in sightings, from one in 1994 to a high of fifty-one in 2006.

"This many sightings and the areas they were reported in (many kilometres east of their habitual range) suggests to us that the bear population is expanding and more bears are being pushed out of traditional areas. We realize that with this type of survey, there will be a percentage of overlap where people at different times have seen the same bear or bears. However, there is also the commonly held belief that for every bear that is seen, there are five to seven bears that are not seen."

Take note that biologists reported the sightings on Caw Ridge went from 1 to 51 in 12 years. Does that indicate they are at the edge of extinction? Look at the contradictions. A couple southwest of Calgary were held hostage in their home last year because a grizzly took up residence in their yard. When they called the authorities for help, they were told to take pictures of the bear.

Photo Leon Lorenz.

I don't care how many bears show up on these studies, there will never be too many; they will always be promoted as a threatened species. Is it not time we threw this threatened species nonsense into the garbage where it belongs?

These surveys plainly show that bears in general are not in trouble. In fact, as woodsmen keep telling us, it is the exact opposite. One thing will be certain—with increasing bear numbers there will be a corresponding increase in aggressive bear behaviour, and we can take that to the bank.

As for BC, it may well be that, like all the discussions going on in Yellowstone Park, it will amount to nothing. Unless they find a way to teach the bears to fear man once again, it may be that the killing of humans has only just begun. As one Yellowstone manager and another bear expert in Alaska stated, "Because of the effects of global warming we may soon become an alternate protein source for the bears."

Another wildlife manager suggested that the bears have to be retrained. They have to know that a rifle shot is not a call to lunch; instead it is a signal to hide. But these managers are facing an uphill battle—all too often public emotions reign supreme.

Is there a possible solution to these problems? I believe so, because it is my belief that responsible outfitters are the best thing that has ever happened where wildlife is concerned. They must conserve and protect healthy game populations or watch their investments vaporize before their eyes. A guiding area without big game is comparable to a café without diners.

The rogue outfitters that did whatever they liked in their often misused guiding territories are becoming as scarce as dinosaurs, and we all know what became of the dinosaurs. The huge investment needed to get into the business means these outfitters have to abide the laws or risk losing everything. Whether we like it or not, these outfitters have become the caretakers of the wilderness. We need to deal harshly with the ones caught abusing their areas, and instead of second-guessing their every move, let's sit back and measure the finished product. If we let them, and the wildlife people, deal with the predators as needed, I believe that in almost all cases we will be pleased with the outcome, as the increase in wildlife will speak for itself.

In areas that remain doubtful, perhaps a bit of controlled burning would help enormously. Let's pay attention to what retired outfitter Dave Wiens noted after they started range burning and brought the wolf populations down—the ungulates and even the birds thrived. The area came back to life. In some instances they have shown hunters up to 100 animals or as many as 30 bull elk in a single day. That is, to put it mildly, an astounding success story.

Because of predator control and range burning, there are more ungulates in some of their guiding territories than ever before in recorded history. Common sense should tell us that their guiding territories are worthless without an abundance of wildlife, yet the guiding territories that sold for $20,000 to $100,000 a few decades ago, now sell for as high as $3 or $4 million. That speaks for itself; that has to be an ultimate truth.

So I remind people that if they eat meat, they are not against killing animals; they are just against killing animals that have a chance of escape. Animals in slaughterhouses do not have that option.

Some people seem to believe that hunting is cruel but the wolf packs are not. I suggest they watch a pack of wolves feeding on a moose that has broken through the ice and is trapped. A CNR train crew watched such a sight at Mile-48 on the Fraser Subdivision. The moose had turned its head around and was watching the wolves tear its insides out. Would we rather see wolves and bears killing the mothers and their newborn, or hunters taking the excess aged animals under the strict control of the Wildlife Branch?

Photo Leon Lorenz.

Remember, all the meat has to be brought out, otherwise a grizzly takes over the carcasses. Since these bears are largely protected, they get first pick. And what becomes of the meat that is brought out? A large part of it goes to food banks to help the needy.

And what about the sources claiming a moose does not feel pain when wolves tear its insides out because they go into catatonic shock? I must question the notion that they feel no pain. Just notice a dog when it is in the jaws of a bigger dog.

I interviewed a man after he was mauled by a grizzly in the Chilcotin country. He went into shock during the attack but he also felt pain. Not just during the attack, but during the following couple of years in the Jubilee Lodge of the Prince George Hospital. Mercifully, death took him away from his suffering, although like many others, his death was not attributed to a bear attack.

Can dreamers change this world into a peaceful place where nothing hurts anything else? How I wish they could. People who drive hundreds of miles in the heat of summer just need to check the fronts of the vehicles and find the enormous number of creatures adhered there. That does not include the endless number of

Photo Steve Schwartz.

creatures crushed along the roadways. Likewise, if you go for a long walk during the summer, try to take note of the great number of creatures you step on, knowing that the ones you see are just the tip of the iceberg. It is the price we pay for existing in nature.

I used to visit a park adjacent to the Fraser River. At times I would sit and watch the nature lovers go by as they enjoyed the view. On nice days the cement walkway was covered with a million ants busy doing their business. It was an eye-opener to watch all the passersby who seemed oblivious to the carnage going on beneath their feet. Just as surprising was the ability of the ants to quickly remove the pieces of their dead and dying relatives.

Does the foregoing appear to be out of context? I doubt it, because the problems wildlife managers are confronted with force them to deal with the reality of nature, and nature can be unspeakably cruel.

I believe we must keep a balance between predator and prey. And most important of all, let's keep the predators on the low side so they will not starve during lean years and have to drag humans screaming from their tents, or stake a claim on some ranch.

At the same time I realize that great care must be exercised in order to prevent ungulates from overgrazing their food supply; obviously a balance is always needed. This will entail never-ending studies and close monitoring. I hope it is apparent the hunters are paying their fair share to support all these conservation efforts.

It is my sincere hope that the public will side with the ungulates and allow more of them to bear their young in peace. A survival rate of 10 percent just shouldn't cut it.

Another point I have to make concerns the people who don't want bears euthanized after they kill humans. Take note that it is just a small step down that slippery slope to not euthanizing them when they eat people. After all, it shouldn't matter because they are dead.

That would make the two gentlemen correct when they suggest that we may become an alternative protein source for the bears. So let's not allow that to happen.

What Charlie Russell and Kevin Van Highem are advocating is that all bears become habituated. If their wishes are fulfilled, then picture wildlife and police officers trying to respond to about 40 calls for help at the same time because bears have invaded our premises. Or worse yet, having these officers tell us to just take pictures of them.

The topper of all has to be the bear expert finding fault with the wildlife officers because they responded to these calls for help. This is absolute madness, folks, so don't fall for it. Bears must be kept *wild*.

The world has changed so much since I was a lad. Back then almost everyone lived close to the land and consequently, close to nature; killing was a necessity of survival. Even my mother had to regularly kill chickens for the pot when we were young. Dad often worked away in logging camps and Mom had to carry an enormous load.

At any rate, you never met anyone who was against hunting back then. But now, because we hire the killing out to slaughter-

Photo Leon Lorenz.

houses that may process (nobody wants to say kill) a million animals a year, we feel we have clean hands. It's an illusion, but it has a profound effect on our interactions with and the views we have concerning wildlife.

Recently 49-year-old Richard White was killed by a grizzly he was taking pictures of in Alaska's Denali National Park. During a one-week period there were seven bear attacks on humans. Abby Wetherell, a 12-year-old girl, was attacked by a bear while jogging. She tried the suggested method of treating the bear right by petting it, but it mauled her. She finally escaped by playing dead.

Perhaps the most pressing question facing us at the moment is this—are grizzly bears dangerous or not? Are Charlie Russell and Kevin Van Tighem correct in their views that we can live safely with grizzly bears if we stop fearing them and treat them right?

Vitaly Nicolayenko and Timothy Treadwell spent the most time around the wild brown bears and their cousins, our wild grizzly bears, and from what I have gathered, treated them royally.

Since they were both killed, I rest my case.

More Non-Fiction Titles from Jack Boudreau

Whitewater Devils: Adventure on Wild Waters

In 1967, in celebration of Canada's 100th birthday, *Les Voyageurs* left Rocky Mountain House, Alberta, in ten 26-foot canoes. These one hundred gallant men, representing eight provinces and two territories, travelled 5,286 kilometres to Expo '67 in Montreal. In his eighth collection, Boudreau shares the stories of the brave and adventurous—sometimes foolhardy—men and women of Northern BC and beyond.

Caitlin Press / 9781894759465 / $22.95 / 2010

Trappers and Trailblazers: More Campfire Stories

In 1934 international entrepreneur and filmmaker Charles Bedeaux hired a team of Canadian men to trailblaze from Edmonton, Alberta, to Telegraph Creek, BC. What started out as adventure for Carl Davidson and Bob Beattie soon became a treacherous and heartbreaking journey. In *Trappers and Trailblazers,* Boudreau has preserved stories in danger of disappearing, and his extraordinary research has also uncovered a collection of intriguing and previously unpublished photographs.

Caitlin Press / 9781894759397 / $22.95 / 2009

Sternwheelers and Canyon Cats: Whitewater Freighting On the Upper Fraser

Forbidding canyons, raging rapids and menacing rocks—this was the daily challenge that faced whitewater men. In the years before the Grand Trunk Railway, these men worked on the wild rivers and creeks to bring freight and supplies to northern BC. This is the story of these "canyon cats," who made their living running the Grand Canyon and other equally dangerous waterways.

Caitlin Press / 9781894759205 / $18.85 / 2006

Wild and Free: Frank Cooke as told to Jack Boudreau

This wild and wooly, scarcely believable but nevertheless true tale of misadventure in British Columbia's northern wilderness portrays the stories of two of Canada's most legendary mountain men—Skook Davidson and Frank Cooke. Together, Boudreau and Cooke reconstruct the memorable life of the "old buzzard," Skook Davidson.

Caitlin Press / 9781894759045 / $24.95 / 2004

Wilderness Dreams

When Clara and Hap Bowden left BC's lower mainland in 1951, little did they know of the adventures waiting for them in the mountains and forests of northern British Columbia. Largely based on forty years of diaries kept by Liza Bowden, *Wilderness Dreams* documents the amazing adventures of the Bowden family in the rugged wilderness of British Columbia's interior, a wilderness they grew to love dearly.

Caitlin Press / 9781894759007 / $19.95 / 2003

Mountains, Campfires and Memories

Champion of the backwoods, Boudreau entertains with more stories from the wilds of British Columbia. Concentrating on the years following the second world war, Boudreau tells us of how men survived, flourished and perished in the northern bush. Adventures gone awry, bizarre encounters with creatures of the woods, missing men and stolen furs were "all in a day's work," as their motto went.

Caitlin Press / 9780920576953 / $19.95 / 2002

Grizzly Bear Mountain

Sequel to bestseller *Crazy Man's Creek*, Boudreau writes of the small community of Penny, BC. Firstly, he recounts the intriguing stories of what the rural kids living there did to amuse themselves (mothers, be warned). Yet most importantly, through Jack's eyes and his developing fascination with the grizzly bear, we begin to understand and appreciate this marvelous beast.

Caitlin Press / 9780920576816 / $18.95 / 2000

Crazy Man's Creek

In this bestseller, Boudreau tells of the men who chose to lose themselves in the rugged McGregor mountain range—long recognized as some of the toughest bush in British Columbia. Life in the mountains included sneak attacks by some of the most ferocious animals, where long winters brought unbearable weather conditions, food shortages and deafening silence.

Caitlin Press / 9780920576717 / $15.95 / 1998